PENGUIN BUSINESS

THE BIG BULL OF DALAL STREET

Neil Borate is deputy editor at *Mint*, where he heads the personal finance team. Neil is a graduate of law and economics. He also has a postgraduate diploma in investments from the University of Birmingham, UK, and has passed the CFA Level 1 exam. He started writing about personal finance in 2016 at Value Research, a mutual fund research portal. After a few stints at fintechs, Neil joined *Mint* in 2019 as a reporter covering mutual funds and other investments. He was made an editor in 2021.

Aprajita Sharma is a financial journalist and has worked across diverse media formats from digital and print to broadcast. She now freelances for *Mint*, *Fortune India*, *Outlook Money*, Kuvera and a couple of mutual fund houses. She has previously worked with *Business Today*, *Business Standard*, *Economic Times* and Zee Business. She covers the stock market and personal finance extensively, including specific beats such as mutual funds, insurance, loans and fintech. She was one among seventeen journalists across Asia who got selected for the Asia Journalism Fellowship in 2021. She is a certified financial planner.

Aditya Kondawar is partner and vice president of key accounts at Complete Circle Capital Ltd, a Delhi-based financial services company. His seven-year financial services sector journey spans investment banking, equity research and entrepreneurship. In his previous role, he was the co-founder and chief operating officer. Aditya is well known in industry circles for simplifying finance and telling stories with a message. He has over 92,000 followers on Twitter and over 15,000 followers on LinkedIn and his articles and views have been covered on all major news sites and blogs. He has been featured on TV channels such as CNBC Awaaz, ET Now and ET Now Swadesh. He has a postgraduate diploma from the National Institute of Securities Ma~'

35

INDIA

Celebrating
Penguin Randon

ADVANCE PRAISE FOR THE BOOK

'The best way to discover the Big Bull. A fast-paced narrative and nuggets of interesting stories with deep dives into some of his picks make this a must-read!'—Radhika Gupta, CEO, Edelweiss Mutual Fund

'I like this book as it resists the temptation of merely amplifying the aura of a revered personality and strives to offer balanced insights into the thoughts and deeds of a man whose exploits are likely to be recounted for generations to come'—Neil Parikh, CEO, PPFAS Mutual Fund

'They don't make investors like Rakesh any more. He was special. A "rare" combination of chutzpah, skill and luck. This book shows you facets of these qualities; especially how he bought Titan in the 1980s and nursed the position for fifteen-plus years before it turned into gold. Or how he suffered margin calls in 2002 and won like a champ after a knock-down. The book is a must-read for the expert and the rookie investor alike. It was a privilege knowing him for decades'—Shankar Sharma, veteran investor, and founder, GQuant and First Global

'The book nicely captures the real person behind the persona. While Rakesh Jhunjhunwala's wins are well-documented and celebrated everywhere, it's interesting to know he also made mistakes and rapidly learnt from them to make himself a better investor and trader. At heart, he remained a student of the market for life'—Vijay Chandok, MD and CEO, ICICI Securities

THE BIG BULL

OF DALAL STREET

How Rakesh Jhunjhunwala Made His Fortune

**NEIL BORATE,
APRAJITA SHARMA
& ADITYA KONDAWAR**

BUSINESS

An imprint of Penguin Random House

PENGUIN BUSINESS

USA | Canada | UK | Ireland | Australia
New Zealand | India | South Africa | China

Penguin Business is part of the Penguin Random House group of companies
whose addresses can be found at global.penguinrandomhouse.com

Published by Penguin Random House India Pvt. Ltd
4th Floor, Capital Tower 1, MG Road,
Gurugram 122 002, Haryana, India

First published in Penguin Business by Penguin Random House India 2023

ISBN 9780143460220

Typeset in Adobe Caslon Pro by MAP Systems, Bengaluru, India

www.penguin.co.in

*To the investors of India, for whom
Rakesh Jhunjhunwala's story is both a dream
and an aspiration.*

Contents

Foreword

Dalal Street is a lane in the Fort area of Mumbai where the erstwhile Bombay Stock Exchange (now BSE Ltd) is located, in Phiroze Jeejeebhoy Towers, a twenty-nine-storey skyscraper.

Of course, with the advent of technology, the physical location of a stock exchange does not really matter much any more, given that the buying and selling of stocks happens online and not in the trading ring of what used to be the Bombay Stock Exchange. Nonetheless, the term 'Dalal Street' is really the metonym for the Indian stock market. This despite the fact that the National Stock Exchange, the bigger of the two exchanges, is located at the Bandra Kurla Complex (BKC) in Mumbai.

Other than the buying and selling of stocks, something that is intricately linked to the idea of Mumbai is the Hindi film industry. Much of the Hindi film industry is based in and around the western suburbs of Mumbai, quite some distance from Dalal Street. And it's perhaps somewhere in these western suburbs that the writers Saurabh Shukla and Anurag Kashyap penned the rather memorable line, '*Mumbai ka king kaun?*', for the film *Satya*.

In the fictional world of *Satya*, the gangster Bhiku Mhatre wanted to be king. But in the real world of buying and selling stocks, Rakesh Jhunjhunwala was the king. And unlike the fictional Mhatre, he didn't need to mouth any dialogues to tell the world that he was the king— *the Big Bull of Dalal Street*. Whenever he did speak, as he often chose to do, investors latched on to every word that he had to say.

But despite the status that Jhunjhunwala had in the Indian stock market and in the minds of Indian investors, there have been next to no attempts made to study him and his investing style in some detail.

In comparison, there are so many books available on the star American investor Warren Buffett. In fact, a lot has been written about other big investors, such as George Soros, Jim Rogers, Peter Lynch, Charlie Munger (Buffett's investing partner), Bill Ackman, etc.

But if you were to log on to Amazon India right now and search for a book on Jhunjhunwala, you are bound to be disappointed in not finding anything good enough to read. Hence, this attempt by Neil, Aprajita and Aditya is indeed very admirable. It's a big first and a good first.

The book does a thorough job of first establishing the human behind the mind and then giving the readers chapters on the stocks that Jhunjhunwala made big money on, including Titan and CRISIL. It also elaborates on his investments, such as DHFL, which went wrong. In that sense, the authors try to maintain a sense of balance and don't fall for the quintessential mistake made by Indian investors and stock market gurus of being bullish all the time.

Also, it needs to be said here that in a world thriving with attention deficiency, the authors do a good job of keeping the chapters short and simple, without making things simplistic.

My favourite chapter in the book is the last one, where the authors tell us what not to learn from Jhunjhunwala. All geniuses have their quirks as well as their weaknesses. In Jhunjhunwala's case, a quirk was his love for leveraged trading, something that not every ordinary mind is built to handle. On the weakness front, Jhunjhunwala loved to drink and did so rather unabashedly. As a Delhi-based stockbroker friend of his puts it in the book: 'He often tried quitting drinking, to the extent that he would admit himself to the hospital, where one cannot drink. But all his efforts were in vain. He would go back to his old habits in just ten to fifteen days.' Further, as the authors point out, 'The passion and discipline he exercised in the investment world were almost completely absent when it came to his health.' And it's this lack of discipline that ultimately led to Jhunjhunwala dying young in August 2022.

To conclude, the authors have rightly focused the book on Jhunjhunwala's investing style and what one can learn from it. Nonetheless, one factor I wish the authors had explored in detail was Jhunjhunwala's habit of equating the success of investing in Indian stocks with the health of the Indian economy, which are two reasonably different things.

One can understand that Jhunjhunwala's interest was in driving up the value of his investment portfolio and to ensure that, he said what he did. But this is not a distinction that the average retail investor, who held on to every word Jhunjhunwala said, has the ability to make.

All in all, this is a great book for every reader who wants to understand why Rakesh Jhunjhunwala was such a success at doing what he did, in the time that he spent in this world.

11 February 2023   Vivek Kaul
Prabhadevi   author of the
Mumbai   Easy Money trilogy
                                   and columnist at *Mint*

Introduction

On 26 January 2023, the Government of India announced that it would posthumously award the Padma Shri to Rakesh Jhunjhunwala. It was recognition of the fact that Rakesh's life was more than a story of stock market success. It provides a template for millions of Indians who are trying to build their own fortune through investing. Wealth creation, from Rs 5000 that he started with in the late 1980s to Rs 35,000 crore at the time of Rakesh's death, stands at the heart of his success story. But there was a lot more to his life than just money-making.

First and foremost, his family values and camaraderie with friends and employees. He would credit his father for all the success he achieved in life. He stayed with his parents until their last breaths. He shared a delightful bonding with his wife, Rekha Jhunjhunwala. His first kid, Nishtha, was born in 2004, after seventeen years of marriage. Twins Aryaman and Aryavir were born in 2009. His friends meant a lot to him. He wouldn't shy away from sharing his stock ideas to help them make money. His employees loved him.

He would give them the freedom to manage his money their way. He wouldn't fuss over losses or boss them around. He would encourage them to take a leap.

Second, the stock market guru preferred the limelight. He would willingly communicate with the media and the public and narrate his own story over and over again, in a lively manner, using colourful language. He wouldn't shy away from voicing his opinions about stocks. He expressed these views even if it made things awkward with fellow celebrities in public discussion forums. His views on Flipkart, expressed on stage with Sachin Bansal present, are emblematic of this.

Third, he was blunt to the extent of often being politically incorrect. 'Pretty women' often featured in his anecdotes. 'I was sitting at my favourite bar, Geoffrey's. A pretty girl asked if I could suggest a stock that will double in three to four years. I gave her the address of Mahalaxmi Race Course,' is a story he often narrated.

Fourth, there was the relative simplicity of his investing style. Rakesh Jhunjhunwala did not expound some complex investing philosophy. He did not shroud his decision behind jargon or claim to have mastery over financial numbers. He attributed a lot of his success to the nation and the growth of India's economy. This was something that ordinary investors too can also capitalize on. These four features of Rakesh Jhunjhunwala's personality made him relatable to thousands of investors even as the stock market was attracting a new generation of Indians. He truly was the pied piper of the stock market.

We couldn't get a chance to meet Rakesh Jhunjhunwala in person. We spoke to as many people as we could—who knew him closely—to narrate his life story. We watched numerous videos of him to compile a first-hand account of what Rakesh Jhunjhunwala would want to tell the new generation of investors. In sixteen chapters spread across three parts, we have encapsulated his early life, his entry into the stock market, jackpot investments and how he picked stocks. We have discussed his failings.

We have compiled his learnings to help readers emulate his style of investment. However, one cannot copy one's way to becoming the next Rakesh Jhunjhunwala. Some traits and techniques were unique to him that made him THE Rakesh Jhunjhunwala. Even his close coterie would be amazed at the way he would handle his investments. The ease with which he would switch between trading and investing was phenomenal. This confidence cannot be copied. The book will take you through Rakesh Jhunjhunwala's early days as a trader and then his journey from being a trader to an investor, which helped him build his fortune.

Flaws are what make us human. Rakesh Jhunjhunwala had his share of flaws. The very discipline in the stock market that made him the king of Dalal Street, the lack of it in his personal life led to his early demise. This book is our tribute to Rakesh Jhunjhunwala. We hope it helps a new breed of investors learn from the best.

Happy reading!

Neil Borate
Aprajita Sharma
Aditya Kondawar

Rakesh Jhunjhunwala's Timeline

1985	Starts with approximately Rs 5000. Borrows money from brother's clients to trade.
1986	Earns about Rs 25 lakh trading shares such as Tata Power.
1987	Marries Rekha.
1986–88	Takes leveraged bet on Sesa Goa based on iron ore prices and rupee depreciation. Capital rises to Rs 2–2.5 crore.
1989	Bullish bet on Madhu Dandavate Budget. Net worth hits Rs 25 crore.
1990–93	Initially bullish and then bearish on the Harshad Mehta market. Successfully times his trades in both directions.
1993–97	Market trades flat. Rakesh does not make significant money.

1997–2000	Dotcom boom. Rakesh misses the 'TMT' or telecom, media and tech boom in India.
2001	9/11 attacks. Rakesh shrugs off worries.
2002–03	Rakesh makes a game-changing, long-term bullish call on India. Buys a big stake in Titan.
2004–07	Rakesh rides the bull run with stocks like Titan, Lupin and CRISIL.
2004	Rakesh's daughter Nishtha born.
2008	Global financial crisis hits. Rakesh's portfolio suffers, but he survives the storm.
2009	Rakesh's twins Aryaman and Aryavir born.
2010	IPO of A2Z Maintenance (a company he invested in) flops. Rakesh's image takes a beating.
2014	Modi victory in election. Rakesh turns bullish, joining the overall market wave.
2018–20	Rakesh makes mistakes on stocks like DHFL.
2020	Rakesh briefly turns bearish in first Covid-19 wave. Quickly reverses his position.
2021–22	Focuses on investment in the unlisted airline, Akasa.
14 August 2022	Rakesh Jhunjhunwala passes away. Net worth estimated at Rs 35,000 crore.

Part I

The Early Years

In this part, we give you a glimpse into Rakesh's early life and how he entered the stock market. We cover his initial days on Dalal Street when he was one among many and how he rose to the top to become the one and only. We introduce to you Rakesh Jhunjhunwala as a family man and as a friend.

Chapter 1

A Chubby Boy

'A sweet, chubby little boy who was very intelligent': Rakesh Jhunjhunwala's older brother, Rajesh Jhunjhunwala, described the younger Jhunjhunwala thus in an interview to Udayan Mukherjee of CNBC-TV18 on Rakesh Jhunjhunwala's fiftieth birthday. 'He is the baby of the family,' he said.

Rakesh Jhunjhunwala was born in Hyderabad on 5 July 1960. His father was an Indian Revenue Service officer posted in Hyderabad. At the age of two, Jhunjhunwala's father shifted to Mumbai and Rakesh spent the rest of his life in India's financial capital. The Jhunjhunwala family was an Agarwal family with a strong Marwadi business ethos and Rakesh's father took an interest in the stock market despite his steady career as a civil servant. This was unusual. In the pre-liberalization era, very few Indians invested in the stock market, with land and gold being the dominant asset classes. In later interviews, Rakesh recounted asking his father why the prices of stocks went up and down. 'Look up news about Gwalior Rayon or Grasim. See what happens to the stock price the next day,' his father would tell him. There was a book, released by the International Labour Organization (ILO), aimed at teaching lay persons how to read company accounts, which Rakesh read at a young age. 'After that, I began reading balance sheets,' he told an audience at the Young Indians Youth Conclave in Mumbai in 2014.

Rakesh studied at Sydenham College in Mumbai and later qualified to be a chartered accountant. 'My father told me to become a chartered accountant because if the stock market career doesn't work out, a CA practice will give a steady income,' Rakesh added at the same event. Chartered accountancy typically involves an extended internship period. 'At the end of it, we become shattered accountants,' Rakesh said with a chuckle. 'You work for three years for Rs 60–80–100 a month. Our seniors would not even give us tea—we would have to pay for the tea,' he said. 'Our conveyance cost was Rs 80. We would make it Rs 150. We could get the extra Rs 70 minus TDS and we would use this for drinks, four times a month,' he recounted, revelling at this little arrangement.

Rakesh's father was ambivalent about his son's chosen career. He told Rakesh not to expect his father to give him any money for stock-market investing but allowed him to stay in the parental home. 'If I didn't go into the stock market, I would have become either a pilot or a journalist,' Rakesh would later recount.

'My father allowed me to pursue a career in the stock market. He told me your word is your bond; be fearless and may God look after you,' Rakesh said in an interview with Ramesh Damani on CNBC (*Wizards of Dalal Street*) in 2002. There was scepticism from Rakesh's mother as well and she reportedly asked him what he would do if he were unable to find a wife. 'That'll be one daughter-in-law less for you to worry about,' he replied, according to a popular anecdote.

Rakesh, the family man and '*yaaron ka yaar*'

Rakesh did get married soon after, to Rekha Gupta, on 22 February 1987. The daughter of Purushotam Premraj Gupta, she came from a rich business family. She effortlessly devoted herself to Rakesh's middle-class family. The couple always stayed with Rakesh's parents. They had three children: Nishtha and twins Aryaman and Aryavir. Notably, the Jhunjhunwalas had their daughter after seventeen years of marriage, in 2004. Their twin sons Aryaman and Aryavir were born on 2 March 2009.

'My parents don't live with me. I live with my parents,' Rakesh would promptly reply when anyone asked if his parents stayed with him. The very statement says a lot about the values he followed in his life. Despite all his riches, he didn't consider moving out of his father's house until his daughter Nishtha was born. Later, the entire family moved to a 4500-sq.-ft duplex in a building called Il Palazzo in South Mumbai's Malabar Hill, one of the most expensive real estate spaces in Mumbai. According to reports, he paid over Rs 25 crore for it. In 2017, he bought another property in Malabar Hill. The fourteen-storey Rakesh Jhunjhunwala house is currently under construction. It will have an area of a whopping 70,000 sq. ft. He also built an 18,000-sq.-ft holiday home in Lonavala as a gift to his daughter.

'I can tell you one thing—nothing is more important to me than my children and there is no woman I can ever love in my life other than Rekha Jhunjhunwala, come what may,' said Rakesh in a TV interview with Udayan Mukherjee on his fiftieth birthday. His privately held equity investment firm RaRe Enterprises comprises two letters each of his wife's and his names—Ra-kesh and Re-kha.

Sharing another anecdote, he said that the day his bullish bet on the Union Budget turned successful in 1990 (more about it in the next chapter), he bought an air conditioner for his wife. Rekha Jhunjhunwala belonged to a rich family before marriage and used to travel in cars when that was still a luxury. She never complained after moving to Rakesh's home. She only had one demand—an AC in the bedroom. RJ fulfilled her demand in an instant when his net worth hit Rs 20 crore after the market rally post-Budget. Not only did he buy an AC for his wife but also for his parents and brother.

'Not a conversation goes by when he doesn't talk about his parents, wife or children,' say his close friends.

A party buff, Rakesh would often throw parties for various reasons. The attendees would be amazed at the way he would organize it all, from invitation cards to food and special party themes. One such was his fiftieth birthday celebration in Mauritius. He managed to fly all his family and friends to the island nation. More than ten personal chefs accompanied him to prepare Marwadi food for the entourage. The party lasted for a couple of days and nights—each day, a new party with a different theme. He had invited celebrity singers and dancers. 'Family and friends did their bit too. The family put together a skit called *Pachas (50) Ke Sholay*. Even his little twins Aryaman and Aryavir participated along with their granny Urmila Jhunjhunwala,' noted a *Times of India* article dated 18 July 2010.

Rekha and Rakesh's twenty-fifth wedding anniversary celebration in 2012 was another occasion when the grandeur of Jhunjhunwala's parties left everyone spellbound. The who's who of politics, the corporate world and Bollywood had marked their presence. But one party that Rakesh loved the most was his parents' fiftieth anniversary on 14 February 2002. For him, it was the most memorable day of his life. 'I booked a suite for my parents and my father said why to waste money and next day when they came back, the way they were flushed, I was so happy,' he told Mukherjee.

Even Covid-19 couldn't tame his zeal. On his sixtieth birthday on 5 July in 2020, he threw himself a *Godfather*-themed party. He had sent out invites that read: 'An offer you can't refuse. You have no choice. No choice at all, my friend. *Capisce?*' It was an online party, of course. 'More than 100 famous people turned up online from various walks of life. He had hired singers to present live shows. People sang, danced and gave speeches,' recalls Samir Arora, founder and fund manager at Helios Capital. Rakesh had also thrown a farewell party for Arora in 1998, when he was moving to Singapore. 'It was at the Trident Hotel in Mumbai. He had gifted me a Laxmi sculpture, which is still with me at my home in Singapore,' Arora says.

A video from his sixty-first birthday party, featuring him in a wheelchair dancing to the song *Kajra Re*, went viral in 2021. Just a month before his demise in 2022, he celebrated his sixty-second birthday at Breach Candy Hospital in July 2022. 'The hospital room was converted into a party room. The food came from four places and he was staying in the hospital suite. He was in a terrific mood,' recalls market veteran Madhu Kela in an interview with Nikunj Dalmia of ET Now.

Friends were equally important to him. They would call him 'Rocky' or 'Bhaiya'. For them, he was an open book. They would call him '*yaaron ka yaar* (a friend among friends)'. He would never hide his stock ideas. 'You walk into his office and his entire portfolio would be out there on screen. He wouldn't shy away from sharing the investment logic of his stock picks,' says a Delhi-based stockbroker friend who had known him since the 1990s. If he identified a great investment idea, he would make sure that his friends also made money from it. The stockbroker friend shares an incident: 'One fine morning, he called me to ready a draft to invest in a stock. He gets upset if you ask him too many questions. I could only ask which stock it was. It was Nagarjuna Construction Company, in which a preferential allotment was to happen. My buying price was Rs 140. In a year, it had fallen to Rs 115. I was losing patience, but I respect him so much that I didn't bother. The stock hit Rs 501 very soon.' Nagarjuna Construction Company is a Hyderabad-based construction and infrastructure firm.

He would help his friends with money without any expectation of a return. He would pay course fees for many of his friends who wanted to pursue law, medicine or architecture but had no money. 'He had bailed out many friends who'd been deep in debt,' recalls a friend.

Arora vividly remembers when, in 2008, Rakesh visited him and told him he had become a billionaire. 'The way he said so was endearing,' he recalls. This was just before *Forbes* had listed him in the Forbes Billionaires List of 2008—for the very first time. Rakesh stood at the thirty-sixth position on the list among the richest people in India, with a whopping net worth of $5.8 billion as of the quarter ending June 2022.

Sharing another anecdote, Arora says Rakesh would often call or message him when Arora gave negative views on television on stocks that he owned. 'It was friendly banter, though. We never saw eye-to-eye on Tata Motors and Delta Corp,' he says.

Relationships were important to him. If he was in hospital, he would note who came to meet him. He would feel bad if someone didn't come. A friend, on condition of anonymity, shares something interesting. Rakesh had strong ideas about why to get in and out of different stocks. But sometimes, personal reasons also triggered stock actions. 'Jhunjhunwala remembered that Delta Corp chairman Jaydev Mody didn't come to visit him in the hospital. He did have other reasons to sell stakes in Delta Corp. But this incident could have been one of them,' his friend says.

Another reason why he may have sold his stakes in Delta Corp is that the company couldn't procure the land-based casino licence in Daman for which it had been waiting a long time. Rakesh never went on record about why he sold his stakes in Delta Corp. Rakesh and his wife together held a 7.48 per cent stake in Delta Corp at the end of the March quarter of 2022. He sold it all in phases in the June quarter.

Another friend says his behaviour had changed post-Covid-19. He was one of the few people who kept buying in the bearish phase right from March. He earned a lot of money in the post-Covid-19 rally. Some say the success finally got to him. 'I could be wrong, but he had turned distant. It had never been so for the thirty or forty years that I have known him,' he says.

One may wonder if his friends nudged him to fix his habits for the sake of his health. They did. But old habits die hard. Rakesh, well aware of his deteriorating health for as long as a decade or more, could not do much to reverse it. Shortly after the birth of his daughter Nishtha on 30 June 2004, in an interview with his friend Ramesh Damani (CNBC-TV18's *Wizards of Dalal Street*), he said that his daughter's birth made him far more aware of his health. 'If I want to spend thirty to thirty-five years with my daughter, being a realist as I am, this is not possible with the kind of health habits I have. If I don't improve, how can I have a good-quality life?' he said.

He could spend only about eighteen years with her.

'He often tried quitting drinking, to the extent that he would admit himself to the hospital, where one cannot drink. But all his efforts were in vain. He would go back to his old habits in just ten to fifteen days,' says the Delhi-based stockbroker friend.

The passion and discipline he exercised in the investment world were almost completely absent when it came to his health. He was visibly sick in his last interview with CNBC-TV18 in the first week of August 2022, but he didn't shy away from the media attention. He even made it to the launch of Akasa Air just a week before his untimely demise. His close friends say he also went to a launch event organized by his mentor Radhakishan Damani just a couple of days before he died.

'He had been acutely sick for the last two years and was often in and out of the hospital. He was extremely frustrated about it. He was not a man who could sit alone, in isolation. He actually felt and believed that he was getting better, but God has his own ways,' says a close friend.

Rakesh summed up his life as one with six major challenges in an interview with his friend Ramesh Damani (about a decade ago).[1] The very first was health. He knew he needed to change his habits in order to live longer and thus spend more time with his daughter Nishtha. Second, spending more time with his parents, wife and daughter. Rakesh lived and breathed the stock market. It was his passion. But he would always try to find ways to be with them.

Third, he was willing to institutionalize RARE Enterprises so that he was not the sole decision-maker. 'For fifteen or twenty years, I have been chairman, peon, clerk, driver—everything of my company. I have a good team of ten people and we have decided to expand it. My skills should live beyond me. I want to give RARE Enterprises a perpetual life,' he says.

Another important change he wished to implement was taking a break from work. He was engaged with the stock market every moment. 'I wish to take one weekend off every month, one week off every quarter, one month off every year. I want to plan it well. I want to see the world,' Rakesh said.

Fifth: kindness. 'God has given me a lot. I should not belittle anybody.' Sixth: charity. 'I am not the owner of my wealth. I am a trustee. I must use my wealth for charity. Mother Teresa says, "Give until it hurts." I pray God gives me the power to do it every year.'

Andrew Carnegie had said, 'The man who dies thus rich dies disgraced.' Rakesh truly believed it. He had pledged to give away 25 per cent of his wealth during his lifetime. Rakesh may not have conquered the first challenge, health. However, he made good progress with the rest of his challenges.

Chapter 2

Entry into the Stock Market

One of the greatest stock-market investors who has ever lived, Rakesh Jhunjhunwala never managed a penny for someone else. Investors the world over would have gladly given him billions for fund management, but the man chose to build his empire through his own money. 'I don't want to be answerable to anyone,' he would often say in interviews. He loved his freedom. 'My wife is my only client,' he would say.

To be sure, although Rakesh may not have entered the asset management business, he did borrow money from individuals in his initial days at high rates—promising them even higher returns than fixed deposits. The self-made billionaire earned his fortunes with his own talent. 'My brother was a practising chartered accountant. He managed to get me a loan of about Rs 20 lakh from his clients. That is how it all started. I earned Rs 25 lakh in the first year of my life in the stock market in 1985–86,' he said.

There is an anecdote that Rakesh began with a capital of Rs 5000. That was, most likely, the amount in his bank account that he had earned during his CA articleship. However, it was the loan of Rs 15–20 lakh from his brother's clients that really allowed him to make his initial returns at scale. Rakesh would elaborate on these early loans in media interviews after he had built much of his fortune. In an interview with investment guru Ramesh Damani, recorded on CNBC in 2011 (*Wizards of Dalal Street*), Rakesh said, 'There was a lady. At that time, FD interest was 10 per cent. I offered investors a return of 18 per cent. I had no security, but I told her after fifteen days I'll give security,' he said, referring to the shares he had bought. Another loan he recounted was from 'a Christian gentleman, Mr Mendonza, who gave a Rs 5 lakh loan'. It seems that Mr Mendonza didn't even ask Rakesh for security against the loan and Rakesh paid him an interest rate of 24 per cent. Rakesh used the money he borrowed from these early loans to invest in the stock market. This is a highly risky practice and a few wrong bets could have easily ended the budding stock market investor's career.

This was the pre-Internet era, when stock-market information was often passed by word of mouth and physically being near the exchange helped. 'I would stand there and talk to people. I never told anyone that my father worked for the Income Tax Department, or they wouldn't talk to me. I used to tell them that he had a clothes shop,' Rakesh later recounted. Interestingly, Shankar Sharma, an investment guru whose career largely coincided with Rakesh's, says that physical presence in the trading ring conferred no real informational advantage. 'I was also a floor trader, we were all active on the floor of the exchange. I don't think it was any advantage. I mean, that was just the method of trading. The real advantage came from knowledge of trading itself, which I think is very important knowledge. Whether you traded physically on the floor or in front of a screen, what's different is only the method of trading,' he said. Despite Sharma's opinion, the physical nature of trading in the late 1980s and early 1990s did allow brokers to get away with high commissions and in some cases, malpractice.

In the mid-1980s, the Indian economy was still highly controlled, with the Licence Raj in effect. A few reforms were underway in sectors such as telephony, but there was no significant wealth creation. The Bombay Stock Exchange (BSE) was the country's largest stock exchange and had a nearly 100-year history. Trading was done manually on the exchange floor and some malpractices were rampant among stockbrokers. Orders were sometimes not honoured and commissions were high, at 3–4 per cent. Clients had to place their orders over the phone and often learnt the price the next day. The opacity of the system allowed brokers to short-change clients by charging higher prices than the actual trade or by declining trades on grounds such as 'signature mismatch'. The BSE Sensex was launched in 1986 with 1977–78 as the base year and a base value of Rs 100. It was in this environment that Rakesh began his investing career.

Rakesh's first stock was Tata Tea in 1986. He bought 5000 shares of Tata Tea at Rs 43 and the stock rose to Rs 143 within three months, multiplying his money three times over. Another one of his early buys was Tata Power.

According to Rakesh, there was a dip in the market after 1986 and he bought 5000 shares of Tata Power, only to watch it recover handsomely. 'At that time, power companies were getting a fixed return as per the Electricity Act. There was some talk of linking it to capacity utilization (the amount of power generated by the company). Tata Power's capacity utilization was 100 per cent. Tata Power would have benefited. I bought it at a price of 150 rupees. There was a dividend of 18 rupees,' he recounted in later interviews. Ramesh Damani, an investor who remained a close friend of Rakesh's over many decades, met him around this time. 'I was extremely fortunate that I had come back from America to start my business. Suppose, on the reverse, you're going to America. And the first week of going to America, you meet Warren Buffett, Charlie Munger, Peter Lynch. It gives you a distorted sense of reality. But that's exactly what happened to me. When I came, I met R.K. Damani, who introduced me to Rakesh Jhunjhunwala. This must have been 1988. It is right at the start of my career,' he said.

In 1986, in his first year in the stock market, Rakesh earned Rs 25 lakh from his stock trading. For the next three to four years, there was no earning. 'They were bear years. I used to go to the ring, but I never speculated,' he later recounted in a conversation with Ramesh Damani.

'The market was bearish. But I was staying with my parents. My wife had a car but we used to go by bus,' he said. Rakesh kept most of his portfolio in Tata Power in this period and earned dividends from this investment, he said in a lecture at FLAME University, Pune in 2013. 'It had a 30 per cent dividend yield,' he added. Dividend yield is the dividend paid by a stock divided by its stock price. The higher the yield, the greater the return in terms of regular income that your investment makes. Ordinarily, an index like the NIFTY or Sensex will have a dividend yield of 1–3 per cent, making a yield such as 30 per cent truly exceptional. Apart from the advantage of living rent-free in the parental home, Rakesh was also financially supported by his family. 'My wife came from a good family. She had her own car. But we used to contribute no money to the household. If my family had not supported me, I would've had to leave the market,' he said in the lecture.

However, his father never gave him a penny to invest in the stock market. During the dry years after his initial success, he eventually went to his father to ask for capital. All he needed was Rs 12 lakh to set up his office. 'I told him I would return the money in the next three years. I felt it was my right to get the money because I had already proven that I can earn profits in the stock market. All I needed was capital,' he said, sharing the story at his special address to young children at the Young Indians Youth Conclave in Mumbai in 2014. He said his father refused to give him money quite sternly. 'You have a right only in your ancestral capital. I am afraid your grandfather didn't leave any,' Rakesh quoted his father as saying.

Chapter 3

Trader versus Investor

Rakesh Jhunjhunwala is on stage addressing a huge audience at a media conclave. The anchor mistakenly calls him a 'stockbroker'. The Big Bull gets visibly miffed. Rakesh certainly was not a broker as he never executed trades or facilitated transactions on behalf of clients. He, in fact, himself traded and invested in stocks. Rakesh began stock trading early in his career. Trading, as opposed to investing, involves a short-term bet on a stock. Traders typically use leverage (borrowing) to magnify their profits. 'My father had told me to never come begging for money. I had to. I had to earn money to invest it. The only way I could have raised capital was by trading,' he would often say. Sesa Goa, an iron-ore mining company, was his first trading bet. The company is now part of Vedanta Ltd. 'There was this fellow in the stock market, Mr Bajaj, who would keep talking about Sesa Goa. He would catch people to convince them about it. Nobody would listen. When he explained the logic to me, I found it attractive,' Rakesh said.

By this time, he had accumulated a capital of Rs 50–55 lakh. He bought Sesa Goa shares worth Rs 1 crore using forward trading (a type of leveraged or debt-fuelled trade). According to Rakesh, the price of iron ore was set in advance and it was going to be 26 per cent higher in the next year. The company would also benefit from rupee depreciation. Rakesh bought 3 lakh shares in Sesa Goa. 'The price went from 26 to 65 in three months and to 2200 in three years. That's how I made the initial money,' he said in a lecture at FLAME University in 2008. Rakesh's capital rose to Rs 2–2.5 crore by the early 1990s.

Another milestone in trading was the Union Budget by Madhu Dandavate, then finance minister in the V.P. Singh government, in the early 1990s. The market was bearish while Rakesh had taken long positions. Long positions are those that benefit when the market rises and short positions are those that benefit when the stock market falls. A long investor is typically called a 'bull' while a short investor is generally called a 'bear'. Dandavate was a socialist and Rakesh felt that the market was unduly pessimistic about the budget. V.P. Singh, the prime minister, had abolished estate duty. According to Rakesh, V.P. Singh was a 'Thakur but also a businessman'. There was talk of a tax on education. Education is a state subject and this would need a constitutional amendment, which is difficult for a minority government, Rakesh later recounted. Rakesh was also confident that V.P. Singh would not allow a very market-unfriendly Budget and he took a leveraged bet on stocks before the Budget. To hedge his position, he shorted some stocks. The confidence paid off. He made a killing. 'I was worth Rs 2 crore on Budget Day. The next day, my net worth amounted to over Rs 20 crore. I staked my life that day,' he said at the Young Indians Youth Conclave. 'The market was bearish. And he was bullish. And it turned out he was right. The market rallied sharply after the Budget,' Ramesh Damani told the authors of this book.

The enormous gains in stock trading also presented a huge tax liability. 'I told my dad I have made around 20–25 crore and the tax was high, around 40–45 per cent. But there was also a wealth tax (which has now been abolished) of 1.5 crore on 25 crore. My dad said why are you so disturbed. Give me your portfolio and I'll pay the tax,' Rakesh later recounted in a public lecture.

During the Gulf War in 1990, Rakesh conducted his first 'short trade'. *The Economist* ran an article with the title 'Has Dalal Street heard of Saddam Hussein?' The magazine wondered why all global markets were falling except India. Until then, he hadn't heard of *The Economist*, but after reading the article, Rakesh went short in the market, he recounted in the 2013 lecture in FLAME University. However, it is not clear whether this trade was successful or not.

At this time, however, the Harshad Mehta boom had started. The Sensex rose from just over 1000 points in January 1991 to cross 4000 points by April 1992—a fourfold rise in just a year and a half. This sort of jump was not backed up by economic fundamentals, even though this period was also the start of (then finance minister) Manmohan Singh's landmark liberalization programme.

Rakesh initially benefited from the rise in stocks but later grew bearish. 'We made money on the rise but we knew it was thievery money. We shorted the market and so when the market came down, we made the money of our life,' he said later in a lecture at FLAME.

'He made a lot of money in the bull market. And then, at some point, he sold and the market kept going up after that. And I think there's a truism that he understood at that stage that being right is not enough. You've got to be right and get the timing right,' said Ramesh Damani.

Shorting is the selling of stocks that you do not own by borrowing them. In return, you pay some interest to the person who has lent you the stocks. You must also return the stocks to the lender by the stipulated time, which means you must buy them back from the market. A short seller hopes that the price of the stock will fall, allowing them to buy it back at a lower price. Short selling is highly risky since a stock can go up to any level, theoretically, and cause unlimited losses to the short seller.

'I took delivery of 14,000 shares of ACC (a cement firm). I remember, we used to fill the transaction forms at night with my clerks. I sold at 3500 but ACC went to 10,000. In 1991, we assessed that this was the best result that ACC will ever produce. Now I have learned that I will not only trade on fundamentals, I would also sell based on the market direction,' he later recounted to Ramesh Damani. There were several instances when Rakesh came close to going bankrupt on his short trades during this period. However, he was saved by the collapse of Harshad Mehta and the bull market that Mehta had artificially propped up. Around this time, Rakesh Jhunjhunwala's net worth was

Rs 100–150 crore. Damani, however, rejects the notion that Rakesh came close to losing it all. 'There is a misconception about this. He had a very strong sense of risk control. People used to think he leveraged a lot but it was within tolerance limits,' he told the authors of this book.

For Rakesh, 1992 to 1999 was a listless period. Short selling was restricted in India after the Harshad Mehta scam in 1993. The bomb blasts in Mumbai in 1993 were a vivid and traumatic recollection for him. He was in the Bombay Stock Exchange at the time. 'That was the only time I felt like leaving the country. Today, if police cannot do anything, tomorrow if someone hurts my wife, who will do anything?' he recounted in an interview with Zee Business in 2014. 'It also turned me into a BJP supporter. We must be really stringent against all this terrorism,' he added.

Market regulator SEBI brought back short selling in 1995, but only for retail investors. Rakesh hung out with his stock market friends and associates for most of the day during this time. 'We used to come to the market at 11 a.m. and talk of the market till 10 p.m. My wife used to say you are not married to me, you are married to each other. We used to go for lunch. Then we would go to our offices for two hours and then we'd have tea. After dinner, the first call was to each other,' he said in a FLAME lecture in 2013. This was a period of introspection and learning.

In 1998, a new bull run began in the stock market. The BSE Sensex rose from just below 3000 to a new high of 5313 in February 2000. However, more than the broad market index, the real action was in tech stocks. Infosys, for example, rose from Rs 11.6 on 1 January 1999 to Rs 172.81 on 3 March 2000. Wipro rose from Rs 13.80 on 1 January 1999 to Rs 257.57 on 25 February 2000.

'Then the tech boom came in which I didn't make much money. I didn't know what software meant,' he later recounted. Rakesh had taken an optional computer course while pursuing chartered accountancy, but he did not complete the course. Rakesh cautiously dabbled in tech stocks, but did not make big bets on them. Nonetheless, he made his mistakes. Rakesh recounted in an interview with the *Telegraph* newspaper that he bought NIIT Technologies in October 2001, only to sell it at a loss a few months later. 'We argued a lot around that time. I was very bullish from 1998 onwards, on the whole,' said Shankar Sharma. 'But he was being more value-oriented. It was hard to justify a lot of the stocks. So any value player would have missed it. Again, that's the constraint you impose when you are a value investor and only buy things that meet certain tests. He had a general value bias, at least back then, and therefore, buying Infosys at 50–60 multiples did not make sense to him,' he added. 'Well, I think from the period of, say 1990 to 2003, the man had accomplished a bit. Yet he was not really a full participant in the telecom-media-tech (TMT) bull run. He didn't quite understand the tech economy that India was building,' Ramesh Damani said.

Rakesh Jhunjhunwala's focus during this time was public sector companies. 'I started buying Bharat Electronics at Rs 18. People were buying tech stocks and used to say "*gadha aya*" (a donkey has come) when they saw me,' he later recounted.

Rakesh also invested in private equity in this period and burnt his hands. His associates had started a fund of Rs 20 crore, of which he contributed Rs 5 crore, he recounted in a 2013 FLAME lecture. 'I lost money but I had the biggest learning of my life. I realized what inhibits growth.

I invested in a company which provides software to hotels. Software at that time cost Rs 4 crore for a five-star hotel. Ours cost Rs 40 lakh. We tried marketing. I even fought with the promoters. Out of the Rs 5 crore, I got Rs 50 lakh back,' he said in the 2013 FLAME lecture. This was not a great period for Rakesh. After having initially avoided sharply rising tech stocks, he rushed into a few at the wrong time. 'I bought a lot of software stocks but I bought them late. I was caught on the wrong foot when the markets went down in 2001,' he later told Ramesh Damani in an interview.

For most of the 1990s, he remained a trader in order to accumulate capital. Using whatever money he earned, he started taking long-term positions in his high-conviction ideas to let the amount grow for compound benefit.

He may have been known as a forever bull, but he accumulated a substantial amount of his wealth by shorting the market in the 1990s. He himself claimed so at various public forums. He made no bones about his trading bets. In fact, his trading strategies had a huge role to play in making him the king of Dalal Street, which status remained till his last breath. He would maintain two separate books—one for trading and another for investing. The investing money was never touched for trading and vice versa. He would take investing bets in the name of RARE Enterprises and trading bets in individual names, be it his own or his wife's.

'That is the journey of most people. The reason why most people start out as traders is because you don't have the capital. We are all first-generation stock-market participants, so trading was the only way out. But once you get the capital, you realize that trading has its place, but it can't be the entire line of thinking. You have to invest. I don't think it was a planned decision but that is the journey he took,' says Shankar Sharma.

Talk to his friends and they would say he was as good a trader as an investor. There are hardly any stock-market investors who can master both like he did. He was extremely sharp at identifying and separating stocks by their trading or investing potential. Very few investors in the world have the acumen to do the best in both.

Rakesh Jhunjhunwala and Harshad Mehta are often portrayed as arch enemies. But even Mehta accepted in private, in front of a journalist, that he was impressed by the fact that Jhunjhunwala could effortlessly do both with equal aplomb. 'We all start as traders and become investors when we have money. 99 per cent traders go bankrupt as they get into investing. I respect Jhunjhunwala (for the fact) that he transitioned from being a trader to an investor and excelled at both,' Mehta told a journalist in private.

Interestingly, he picked his most profitable investment at the beginning of his stock-market career, in his trading days. There's a popular story about Rakesh Jhunjhunwala buying the stock of Titan Industries in 2002 at Rs 3. At the time of his death, the stock price was Rs 2472, implying a stratospheric gain of 824 times in a twenty-year period. The story burnishes the myth of a stock-picking genius— buying at the bottom and holding to the top. However, the reality is a little different. Anil Manchanda, a former vice president at Titan and a director at the Tata Share Registry, wrote an article in the *Hindu Business Line* on 14 August 2022, in which he described how Rakesh had actually started buying Titan in the mid-1980s. While he saw some swift gains in that period, the company went into the doldrums in the 1990s. The stock saw a major revival in the post-2002 period and Rakesh profited from it. However, the image of a perfect bottom-picker is busted. Instead, Rakesh's fortune from Titan is a testament to his ability to wait and to repose faith in the management of what was to eventually become a multi-bagger company.

'Shortly after Titan Co. Ltd (then Titan Watches) shares got listed in the mid-1980s, Tata Share Registry, the company that handled shareholder accounting for most of the listed Tata companies, realized that Rakesh Jhunjhunwala, then an up-and-coming stock market operator, was accumulating Titan shares in huge numbers and had, in fact, become the largest single individual shareholder, leaving Ratan Tata and other Tata directors far behind. Tata and Titan executives had never heard of this man. They could not figure out what was happening or what he was up to and why,' Manchanda wrote. 'An emergency conclave of concerned Tata directors and Titan executives followed. Nimesh Kampani, head of Titan's merchant bankers, J.M. Financial Services, was tasked with informally approaching RJ and ascertaining his intentions. RJ said he was flattered by the Tata interest in his activities but had no intention other than to put his money into what he thought was much more than a mega multi-bagger. He said he was in it for the long haul and would stick with the stock through thick and thin,' Manchanda adds.[1]

According to Manchanda, Titan was trying its hand at international markets, and failing. 'It turned out that the Swiss and the Japanese competitors were cut from a different cloth than the hapless HMT and Allwyn. When confronted by real competition, Titan found it had no genuine strength and plenty of weaknesses,' Manchanda wrote. 'Eventually, when the change of guard happened naturally, Tatas quickly wound up international operations. The gold price also took off, and the success in the jewellery business sent the stock soaring again, way beyond the wildest imagination of Titan's founding team and the Tata Group. Through all this Rakesh Jhunjhunwala stuck on; eventually reaping a bounty which he once admitted was even beyond his most optimistic expectation.' According to Shankar Sharma, trading gives a person an eye for detail. In trading, positions are leveraged and short-term price movements matter a great deal, so you cannot afford to miss anything. Those with the invest-only mindset (often mutual fund managers) miss out on the skills that trading imparts. Rakesh's trading made him a better investor, according to Sharma.

Chapter 4

Weathering Storms—Dotcom Bust to Great Recession

Rakesh Jhunjhunwala was not as famous as the likes of Harshad Mehta, Manu Manek, Radhakishan Damani, Chandrakant Sampat, Ketan Parekh and others in the 1990s. He was one of many on Dalal Street. He rose to fame at the start of the twenty-first century. While most investors lost money when the tech boom burst in 2000, Rakesh remained unaffected. 'Neither did he make money in tech stocks, nor did he lose much when the tech madness roiled the markets,' says his investor friend.

Along with the dotcom bust came the 11 September attacks in the US. Rakesh was shaken by it. 'After the 9/11 attacks happened, I didn't leave my room for seven days. I used to get up, watch TV and go to sleep,' he later said in a video interaction. However, Rakesh soon recovered from this shock. 'The market went down . . . and the way it rebounded! Indian companies had a lot of unutilized capacity. Interest rates were low. Inflation was low. Can you believe a stock like Greater Eastern—Rs 25 price, Rs 57 book value, Rs 85 freight value, Rs 3 dividend?' According to Rakesh, stocks became available at throwaway prices. 'I could buy Praj for Rs 100 and Nagarjuna for Rs 13,' he said in the 2013 FLAME lecture. 'One time I got Rs 25 lakh Telco shares between 260 and 270 and seven days later I sold it between 330 and 340. That time, there were opportunities in trading also,' he said.

After the dotcom bust of 2001, Rakesh gradually changed his style, from short-term trading to more long-term investing, and this laid the foundation for a spurt in his wealth in the coming boom of 2002–07. However, he continued to employ leverage to magnify his returns and indulge in short-term trading on the side.

Eventually, however, the market turned. The Sensex rose from around 5000 points at the start of 2004 to top out at around 20,000 in January 2008. Rakesh made huge money between 2004 and 2008 and that is the period during which the media labelled him as the 'Big Bull of Dalal Street'. However, by 2007, valuations across the world (including India) were looking stretched. 'I got bearish on the market from October to November 2007,' Rakesh told his interviewer at Zee Business in 2014. 'I was sure that there was going to be a fall not only in India but in all asset classes worldwide. I said so and made presentations about it. I thought it will be severe but I didn't expect the NIFTY will go below 4000. The fall below Rs 4000 also shocked me,' he said. 'In hindsight, there is a certain class of companies that can only be sold in bull runs. You should use the opportunity of extreme bull runs to lighten your positions. In any large bull runs of thirty-forty years, there are going to be major corrections. Whenever markets take momentum towards a side—either up or down, the leverage is not known. Market can be extremely optimistic on the upside and extremely pessimistic on the downside. That's where you get the great opportunity,' he said. 'If the government allows capital account convertibility, I want to try and do what I do in India, on an international scale,' he added, when asked about his future ambitions in that interview.

In 2008, a global economic crisis began with the collapse of Lehman Brothers in the US. The mortgage market in the US was at the epicentre of the crisis, but it quickly spread to Europe and India. The NIFTY dropped from around 6200 in January 2008 to less than half of that at 2700 by December 2008.

Sanjay Pugalia, then a journalist with CNBC Awaaz, interviewed Rakesh on 25th December 2008.[1] 'What's your outlook for the next one year?' Pugalia asked. Rakesh's answer was somewhat enigmatic. 'I have two activities— trading and investment. For investment, I have a horizon of more than two–three years. For trading, I keep all opinions at home. In my life, there is never any price target for trades. How do I know? I see the screen, the screen talks to me.' However, Pugalia persisted in trying to elicit Rakesh's stance on the stock market. 'Those who accepted investing for the long term are in losses. Those who traded seem to be in profit. For 2009, isn't trading a better strategy?' he asked. Rakesh answered with his characteristically bullish stance. 'I don't think so. Now is the time to buy the riskiest assets. Risk is a word with many dimensions. But the way I see it—say I buy something for Rs 100. Could be that it becomes 60 or 70 or 40. But the way I envisage things, can it be 1200, can it be 1300, can it be 500 or 400? What is the probability of the asset reaching those prices? I think the riskiest assets bought now can give you the greatest return provided you have the risk appetite, patience and it's your own (not borrowed) capital. I have thought many times—why should I not invest outside markets or why should I not run a business? Where the hell do I get 15–16 per cent tax free returns? Return in India cannot be below nominal GDP growth. Normally, they are 1.5x nominal GDP growth. Invest with reasonable expectations of 15–18 per cent. There is also easy liquidity in case of stock markets,' he said.[2]

Rakesh's wealth creation was helped by a favourable tax regime on stock market investments in India, which exempted long-term capital gains (LTCG) on equity from taxation. The tax structure existed in the first decade of the 2000s (since 2004), as well as the second, until the 2018 budget introduced the long-term capital gains tax. 'I have a friend in the Middle East who asks me, what is income tax? I also say the same thing when people ask me—what is income tax? Long-term capital gains and dividends from stocks are tax-free,' he told the audience at the CII event in 2014. Both these concessions have now been abolished. The year 2018 saw an imposition of 10 per cent capital gains tax on long-term capital gains above Rs 1 lakh. The 2020 Budget made dividends fully taxable, at an investor's slab rate.

After staging a rebound in the 2009–10 period, India's economy and stock market were again beset by a crisis in 2011. Inflation surged to double digits as too much money was spewed out by central banks to combat the recession. However, global supply had not kept up. India was particularly affected by this crisis, with the government's fiscal splurge coinciding with the easy-money policies of the RBI. Rakesh was present on a panel discussing Motilal Oswal's 16th Wealth Creation Study. He reiterated his long-term optimism about India, even as fellow panellists such as Raamdeo Agrawal of the Motilal Oswal Group and Ramesh Damani seemed pessimistic. The scenario was eerily similar to the inflation worries that would plague the world again in 2022. Rakesh, however, took the position that supply would eventually catch up with demand and the commodity price rises behind the global inflationary surge would be temporary. He also saw a silver lining to India's large budget deficit.

'If you look at India's GDP this year, it will be 70–80 lakh crores. The cumulative deficit of the states and Centre would be 8–8.5 per cent. The extent to which you are incurring capital expenditure, it would not be inflationary immediately because it will build supply. The extent to which you are using deficits to fund consumption, that would be the biggest source of inflation. You're going on increasing employees' salary in the government—the employees are getting buying power, how do you get the supply? The real source of the inflation according to me is the budget deficit and commodity prices. One thing that is assumed in commodity price inflation is that demand will be same at all levels. That may not be correct. There will be substitutes. If you look at the return on capital that companies are getting in the present commodity prices, why will supply not come? Look at the amount of profits that companies like Rio Tinto are earning. I'm not a commodity bull (to think) that commodities will go up, day by day, year by year,' he said. 'A lot of the bears have been telling me that 5200 will be the high-water mark for the NIFTY. What's your view?' Ramesh Damani questioned him. The answer was delivered in Jhunjhunwala's trademark folksy style. '*Dekh*, Ramesh, *zindagi mein har aadmi ka din aata hai* (every person has his moment). So be it. I only want to know at the end of five years, their balance sheet and my balance sheet. I think markets are in a difficult place, we could be in a range for a long time. But I have no qualms that I should sell my equity and invest elsewhere and India will not grow. I am confident. A lot of pessimism is getting priced in,' he said.

Damani persisted, trying to pierce Rakesh's optimism. 'Do you feel we are actually going to create a 10 trillion economy in thirty years?' he asked.

Rakesh chuckled. '10 trillion in twenty-five years! We are already at 2.5 trillion USD. If we don't get there, I'll commit suicide, yaar. I just read a note by Standard Chartered which says 30 trillion in thirty years. We want labour reforms, GST, DTC, FDI in more areas. It'll happen in one to two years. The country's not going to end tomorrow if GST doesn't come. More transparent and speedier decision-making. It's not like India's gone to the dogs,' he said.

Rakesh thus stayed put throughout the years of economic stagnation and relatively muted growth in 2011–13. In 2014, with Narendra Modi's victory in the general election, the stock market rallied. On the eve of the landmark Modi victory, Rakesh attended an event organized by ValueQuest (a portfolio management company). Again, he was questioned about his enthusiasm for a country that had seen three years of stagnation and policy paralysis as scandals hit the government of the day.

'Why are you bullish on India?' he was asked.

'Ask yourselves one question—are the problems of India structural or cyclical? India's grown at a faster pace in every decade since Independence regardless of the problems the country has faced. To my mind, the problems are largely cyclical. What are the problems? Corruption, mismanagement of state resources and having social welfare faster than you can afford it. I'm confident that BJP will get not less than 200 seats . . . I'll consider myself and India unlucky if BJP doesn't win. If he wins, in the wave of optimism, he will be able to do a lot of things,' Jhunjhunwala replied.

'Titan went from Rs 1600 in 2008 to Rs 600 in 2009. That time you didn't feel like selling Titan?' came another question.

'You have an entry value and an exit value. If I feel that the original story due to which I entered is still alive, why would I exit the stock?' Rakesh answered.

'So you'll hold it for ten–twenty years?' the questioner persisted.

'I hope to hold it till 2020. After that, I don't know what I'll do. I'll give you the example of Lupin. Lupin gave no return between 2006 and 2008. But it has been the best performing stock from 2008 to 2013. I feel Titan has given me such a great return—if it gives me 15 per cent, what's wrong?' came the answer.

His bullish stance on India was such that in his last interview to Shereen Bhan of CNBC-TV18, where he looked visibly pale and debilitated, he talked about India's growing per capita income, and the resulting boost in discretionary expenditure, in his feeble yet passionate voice. This was the very reason why he saw Akasa Air doing well. He was an early investor and also the owner of the airline. 'I see India growing at 10 per cent. I feel confident about India's aviation growth story. There will be a lot more flights. Akasa will be a very competitive airline. We are not a low-cost but a frugal airline,' he says.

He shared his views on the markets as well as his view of central banks across the world raising interest rates. 'The markets will grow but at a slower pace, regardless of global developments,' he adds.

While other Big Bulls Harshad Mehta and Ketan Parekh faced a terrible end, how was Rakesh able to stay away from controversies? A few incidents have clouded his career, but no large-scale insider trading charge or fraud was proven. People close to him testify to skill being responsible for his success rather than underhand deals.

What about insider trading charges? In September 2021, Rakesh did a bulk deal in Zee Enterprises days ahead of the Board of Directors of ZEEL unanimously providing in-principle approval for the merger between Sony Pictures Networks India (SPNI) and ZEEL. He earned over Rs 70 crore in a short span. Murmurs about insider trading arose. However, a close friend, whose fund house is invested in Zee Enterprises, confirms this wasn't the case. 'Had it been true, I would have surely known, me being his close friend and my fund house a big investor in the stock,' says his investor friend.

In another incident, 'Rakesh and others settled an insider trading case related to Aptech by agreeing to pay Rs 37 crore under the consent route, according to which an individual can close a pending matter without admitting or denying the charges.'[3] 'I think this was just a matter of unintentional non-disclosure that led to insider trading charges,' his investor friend said on condition of anonymity.

Another associate explains this issue. 'Many of us deeply involved in the stock market sometimes get information. The information alone does not help. You need the skills to make use of it. No investor can grow as big as he did only because of insider trading,' he said.

Chapter 5

Investment Musings

Rakesh was an optimist. He firmly believed in the India story. One of Rakesh's most famous calls was one in 2002— that India was on the cusp of a long structural bull market. He wrote an op-ed in the *Economic Times* titled 'India—At the Threshold of a Structural and Secular Bull Market' in June 2002, when the Sensex had hit 3000. It was a period of gloom and doom. Investors were surprised and shocked at his optimism. But he believed in India. Interestingly, this turned out to be too early a call on the coming bull market. 'Rakesh turned bullish in 2002, but the market kept falling in 2002 and 2003. These years were very hard on him because leverage magnifies losses as well as gains,' said Shankar Sharma. Rakesh himself alluded to this mixed journey in the early 2000s in a TV interview. 'My call was very good at the Sensex of 3000. I got extremely bullish in 2002 December and the market took off in 2003 March– April. For about twelve to eighteen months, I carried the highest leverage of my life. There was a setback in 2002 June. I had to liquidate 25 per cent of my portfolio in four days. But I did that, I honoured everything. When the markets turned favourable again, I leveraged again,' he said in a conversation with Ramesh Damani on CNBC in 2020.

It was in these confusing early 2000s that Rakesh bought some of the stocks that built most of his investing fortune over the next two decades. Although Rakesh had Titan in his portfolio for a considerable period since the 1990s, it is possible that he significantly added to the Titan investment at this time, when the stock was trading at Rs 30–35 levels. What made him buy it? According to Damani, it was a mixture of intuition, impulse and research. 'The thing that people will find hard to understand is that he was an "investigate later, buy now" kind of guy. In the sense that he had a gut feel. That's not completely true, because he was a man who was 24/7 dedicated to the market. So he did study companies, sectors and the markets all the time. The way the transaction happened, as he told me, was that a broker offered him 20 lakh shares, you know, at 20–40 rupees. He was bullish on it, looking for good companies to invest in the consumer space. So he closed the deal,' Damani said.

In 2003, Rakesh and his wife also bought their first significant stake in CRISIL, buying 10,000 shares. United Breweries was another buy at that time. In subsequent speeches, such as one at a CII event in 2004, Rakesh outlined his philosophy. Essentially, it was a mixture of fundamental investing principles and a bullish view on India. 'Lot of people think that I have an investment philosophy. I have an investment approach. The first thing I look for is opportunity. Without opportunity, there can be no economic activity and without economic activity, there can be no profit. When I look at Colgate, I look at the present demand for toothpaste in India and what it can become. Infosys became Infosys partly because of what it was but also (because) the Internet and use of tech were key ingredients. I made a lot of money in a company called Praj Industries. Why? It had an ethanol plant. The opportunity for ethanol just went through the roof,' he said.

According to Rakesh, his stock-picking follows a four-pronged process. 'First, I look for opportunity. Retail is an industry with the highest opportunity. I want to invest where demand naturally exists. I invested in Rallis because there is no question that use of pesticides and seeds has to go through the roof because increase in food production needs production of those inputs. Next, I look for competitive advantage. I try to zero (in) on a company's competitive ability and what it already has in relation to the opportunity before it,' he said. 'Third, my friend asked if I should invest in large cap or small cap stocks. I said you should invest in small cap companies which can become large cap. I invested in Titan at Rs 500 crore and it is now Rs 11,000 crore,' he added. 'Fourth, understanding liquidity is extremely important. You should not have more than 5–10 per cent of the outstanding stock of any company. Otherwise liquidating it will be very difficult. Whatever you eat, you must be able to push out the other end,' he said in a lecture at FLAME University in 2013.

Despite this cleverly articulated strategy, Rakesh sometimes acted on impulse.

In a 2014 interview with ValueQuest, he elaborated on his choice of DHFL, a company that went bust in 2019, hurting Rakesh's portfolio. 'Nothing is done scientifically. It is done intuitively and nobody participates in the final decision—none of my partners and none of my research people. I decide on the spot.' Rakesh was quite picky about people he would meet for investment pitches. After many requests, he agreed to meet the founder of an electronics manufacturing services provider based in Delhi. The founder was the husband of a famous Bollywood celebrity. His pitch lasted for an hour and Rakesh declined to invest in less than a minute. He did explain the reasons why his business would not be successful. 'The founder agreed later on the call—that what RJ was saying was all true,' says the stockbroker friend.

The business indeed failed.

He was also a quick decision-maker. Madhu Kela shared a similar story in his interview with Dalmia of ET Now. Kela met Rakesh at his Fort office in Mumbai in 1998. He was working with a broking house, Peregrine Securities, as a salesman. 'Honestly speaking, I knew nothing about investing. I had prepared the spiel that the liquor business is going to grow very big and I am giving 5 per cent in all the companies for only Rs 15 crore. He asked me where have I come from. I said I work in Peregrine, one of the largest broking houses. I am the chief dealer there. He made me sit and he said okay, deal closed,' says Kela. This happened in a matter of thirty minutes.

His conviction in his long-term investments would often shock those around him. '*Bhaiya*, it hasn't rained this year. The Escorts share price is already down and the results too are bad,' Rakesh's team told him (as recounted by a stockbroker friend). '*Is saal baarish nahi hui toh kya? Agle saal ho jayegi* (doesn't matter if it didn't rain this year. It'll happen next year),' he calmly responded within seconds. Escorts is an engineering conglomerate that manufactures agricultural tractors and construction equipment, among other machines.

His conviction in Escorts (now Escorts Kubota) was exemplary. He had first invested in the company in August 2013 and increased his stake subsequently in 2014 and 2015. This is because it was at a time when no banker or private investor was ready to offer the company a loan. 'When I asked him about his Escorts bet, he told me he saw fire in Nikhil Nanda. He was convinced Nanda was driven to turn the business around,' says his friend.

Rakesh was proven right. He invested in the company when the stock was trading below Rs 100. In just five years, in 2018, the stock breached the Rs 1000 mark. The company used to be a blue-chip engineering firm. A foray into telecom and healthcare didn't quite work out for the Nanda family. Rakesh backed the company when it was drowning in a pile of debt and fresh lending seemed impossible. 'I felt certain that Jhunjhunwala was making the wrong decision, but the risk paid off,' his friend says.

Cash flows mattered to Rakesh. He brutally grilled Flipkart co-founder Sachin Bansal at a panel discussion organized by the Retailers Association of India in 2016. 'Fortune 500 companies have been built by cash flows and profits and not with investors' money. The round 1 and round 2 is fine, but no Fortune 500 firm has gone for round 3 or 4. Secondly, all Fortune 500 (companies) pay taxes, unlike online players. Great businesses are made with skills and superior business models,' Rakesh said.

Bansal did defend himself that day, but the rest is history. The US-based retailing giant Walmart acquired a 77 per cent stake in Flipkart for $16 billion in 2018. Sachin Bansal, who had co-founded the company with Binny Bansal in 2007, exited the company.

Rakesh was later criticized for his apathy towards new-age businesses that were launching initial public offerings (IPOs) in 2021. RJ stuck to his basic investment principles of profitability and cash flows. Eventually, he was proven right with the kind of tech rout that happened at the beginning of 2022. Many of the new-age tech IPOs are still trading below their IPO prices. 'The way fathers tell their sons "all this money is yours", similarly, new-age businesses talk about making money. *When*? That is the question,' Rakesh quipped.

Private bets and the Bollywood connection

Rakesh got his Midas touch in private investment quite late. In 2021, he accepted that half of his investments in unlisted companies failed. 'I made about twenty private equity investments (in unlisted companies). Out of these, ten are duds—they are written off. Five of them gave moderate returns, and the remaining five have done beautifully,' he narrated at the India Economic Conclave 2021. However, he was quick to add that he made better returns in private equity investments than in listed companies.

Take, for example, Nazara Technologies, a gaming and sports media platform. Rakesh invested Rs 180 crore in Nazara in 2018, according to reports. The stock was eventually listed in the stock market in 2021. His investment value grew nearly three times in three years. Rakesh still holds 10 per cent stake in the company, as of the quarter ending September 2022.

Another successful investment is Star Health and Applied Insurance. It took him eighteen years to close the deal in the company. He acquired his 14.98 per cent stake in the company in a staggered manner between March 2019 and November 2021. The company was listed in December 2021. According to the red herring prospectus, his average purchasing price for Star Health was 155.28 per share. The stock hit its all-time high of Rs 940 on 10 December 2021.

Metro Brands (previously known as Metro Shoes) is another investment worth mentioning. It is a multi-brand footwear retail chain in India. Rakesh invested in it in 2007. He held 14.43 per cent stake in the company as of June 2022. The company's shares got listed in the stock market in 2021.

Another unlisted investment, Concord Biotech, has filed its draft red herring prospectus with SEBI. The company is an active pharmaceutical ingredient (API) maker. RARE Enterprises owns a 24.09 per cent stake in the company.

Bollywood is an integral part of Mumbaiwallahs' lives, and it was no different for Rakesh. He forayed into Bollywood as a producer. His first movie as a co-producer was the Sridevi-starrer *English Vinglish*. He co-produced it with adman-turned-filmmaker R. Balki and Radhakishan Damani. The film was a big Bollywood success.

He later produced *Shamitabh* and *Ki and Ka*. His latest release as a co-producer, *Chup*, came out in September 2022. What's common to all these movies is the presence of R. Balki either as a producer or a director. Another movie, *Ghoomer*, starring Abhishek Bachchan, Shabana Azmi and Saiyami Kher, is yet to release.

'Rakesh Jhunjhunwala didn't even hear the script of *English Vinglish* before backing it. He just said, "If you are making it, I am on." I asked him, "Won't you like to hear the story before coming on board?" He replied, "No. If you are making it, it has to be worth it, right?" That's the kind of equation we had with him. He never questioned me. He didn't really make a lot of money through films and yet, he was in this business for the passion of cinema,' Balki told Bollywood Hungama.[1]

Rakesh was also the chairman of Hungama Digital Media Entertainment Pvt. Ltd.

Many people would remember various actresses, from Priyanka Chopra, Nargis Fakhri, Deepika Padukone and Katrina Kaif to Alia Bhatt, in conversation with Rakesh on Diwali day on TV channels.

Part II

The Successes and Failures of Rakesh Jhunjhunwala

In this part, we highlight three stocks that built Rakesh Jhunjhunwala's fortune—Titan, CRISIL and Lupin—and three mistakes that Rakesh Jhunjhunwala made—DHFL, A2Z Maintenance and Mandhana Retail. We give you the stories of these companies and of Rakesh Jhunjhunwala's investments in them. Read on.

Chapter 6

The Story of Titan

The journey of a thousand miles begins with a single step, and the journey of Titan began with one watch. Today, every three seconds, someone somewhere around the world buys a Titan watch. Titan started in 1984 with just one product category—watches. Xerxes Desai, a senior executive with the company, was looking for new business opportunities for the firm when he chanced upon the idea of watch manufacturing in 1977. The Titan story is documented in detail in the book *Titan: Inside India's Most Successful Consumer Brand* by Vinay Kamath, published in 2018, parts of which we will rely upon, along with Titan annual reports, in this chapter.

After almost a decade of tenaciously navigating through the public-sector Hindustan Machine Tools' (HMT) hegemony, the reluctance of the Swiss to part with watchmaking technology, the Licence Raj and RBI's stringent forex norms, Titan was formed as a joint venture between the

Tamil Nadu Industrial Development Corporation (TIDCO) and the Tatas in 1984. TIDCO had been looking at a few projects and its talks with other watchmakers hadn't borne fruit. To provide much needed foreign exchange to finance the purchase of the required capital equipment, assistance was sought from the International Finance Corporation (IFC), based in Washington DC. The IFC is the private sector-focused sister entity of the World Bank. The IFC was so enamoured by the project, it even sought to make an equity investment in Titan.

Titan chose to locate its first plant in Hosur and its headquarters in Bangalore. The fact that HMT's watch plant was located in that city was a major incentive. Xerxes said as much in an interview published in *Businessworld* magazine in December 1989. The main reason for choosing Hosur was its proximity to Bangalore. They thought it would be easier for them to pull people out of HMT especially the ones with technical and managerial experience. They wanted to raid HMT and they were successful with the same. It was a blessing in disguise for them as HMT was overflowing with staff and the growth avenues at the top-level management weren't many, which made the raiding even easier.[1]

Titan launched with five watch collections: Exacta (steel), Fastrack (sporty models for the youth), Classique (gold-plated dials with leather straps), Spectra (two-tone—steel and gold) and Royale (gold-plated dials with gold-plated metal bracelets). The lowest priced was Fastrack, at Rs 350, and the highest was Royale at Rs 700. From day one, Titan was projected as a premium brand. That first day at the Safina Plaza showroom, Titan sold seventeen watches;

the first month's sale was 313 watches. The Classique range was the bestseller, accounting for 65 per cent of sales.

However, the journey was not without its hiccups. From the initial batch of Titan watches manufactured in December 1986, J.R.D. Tata was gifted a watch. To the embarrassment of the Titan team, the quartz watch given to Mr Tata was not working. In the 1990s, Titan took the disastrous decision of entering the European market. Used to working in a monopolistic environment in India, Titan was unable to match up to the exacting standards of delivery and quality that watch retailing in Europe involved. It was a struggle, recalls Ajoy Chawla, a young manager in the early 1990s who would later head new business incubation and strategy for Titan Company Ltd, even to pay salaries and the rent for the premises. The effect was very clear on the financials—despite growing revenue from Rs 700 crore in 2000–01 to Rs 800 crore in 2002–03, net profit decreased from Rs 23.5 crore in 2000–01 to just Rs 11.5 crore in 2002–03. Titan was going through a tough phase. It was a trying time for Bhaskar Bhat, who took over as managing director in 2002.

The management was asked to come up with a winding-up plan and bring back the stock and whatever cash remained. It was a difficult period: the audit committee had TIDCO representatives and there was a great deal of mistrust and suspicion. Finally, in 2004, a couple of years after Xerxes Desai had retired, the European operations were brought to a stop. The accumulated losses added up to Rs 182 crore and it took several years for Titan to wipe it off the balance sheet. While Indian operations continued to be profitable—Titan made Rs 21 crore in net profit in

2004–05 and Rs 99.9 crore in 2006–07—the overhang of the European losses troubled the company for a long time. Xerxes Desai had seen success in the Indian market, while the European foray was a failure. However, a catalyst for Titan's turnaround was the entry of Bhaskar Bhat as its MD on 1 April 2002.

When Bhat took over the reins at Titan, the company's market value was a mere Rs 220 crore, a tenth of Tata Power's and around one-fifteenth of Tata Steel's and Tata Motors'. Now, Titan is valued at Rs 2,18,000 crore. It is the second-largest Tata company in terms of market capitalization, after Tata Consultancy Services. Moreover, between 2001–02 and 2018–19, Titan's revenues and profits grew at an annual rate of over 20 per cent and 30 per cent, respectively.[2]

It is unclear exactly when Rakesh Jhunjhunwala first entered Titan. But it is confirmed from a video interview that he made a significant purchase around this time, in 2001–02, at a price of Rs 30–32 per share.

The Big Bull in an interview said, 'I didn't know zilch about Titan. One day I was sitting, I was very bullish, a broker called Daaki called me. He said five lakh shares of Titan, which were trading at Rs 34, were available to him at Rs 32. I called my friend Lashit, he said not to buy it as Morgan Stanley was expected to sell 90 lakh shares and that I will get it cheaper. But I didn't listen to him and bought those 5 lakh shares and slowly accumulated 12.5 lakh shares. I thought not to leave the shares despite Lashit's view. When the stock reached Rs 43–44, I went to meet the managing director of Titan, Bhaskar Bhat. I had gone to many Tata offices, but this one was totally different. All young people, vibrant office space, etc. I had a meeting at 6 p.m. Bhaskar Bhat was so respectful, disciplined and dedicated that he came at 6 p.m., but due to some union meeting, he said he will be late by thirty minutes. He gave me a conference room to sit in. He came at 6.45 p.m. and the meeting lasted for four hours till 10.45 p.m., where I was explained everything about the company and the approach. He told me honestly that the task is difficult but they will do it. Bhaskar's wife called six times and finally he told the secretary to pass the phone to him.'

'I look at the sheer size of the opportunity and I also tend to invest in what the market tends to ignore. Because I think, in investment, that's where the greatest opportunities lie. I may be a momentum player as far as trading goes, but where investments are concerned, I don't believe in momentum at all. Investments should be in those areas which the market does not favour,' Rakesh said in a Capital Ideas Online conference in the year 2000.[3]

When asked how he built conviction on the Titan stock, he said that he bought the stock at various stages at a price range of Rs 32–125. 'You cannot create a Titan company. When India booms and it will, their margins will go up from 10 per cent to 14 per cent (FY20 margins were 10 per cent and FY22 margins were 12 per cent for Titan). I have never seen a company that has such integrity. Right now, it is a difficult period for them, but they will re-create themselves. Even when the price from Rs 1600 in 2008 fell to Rs 600 in 2009, that didn't shake his confidence as he said India will grow at double digits and the best is yet to come,' he added in an interview with ValueQuest.

He said he will live to see that day and then that day will be the time to sell Titan.

How Bhaskar Bhat won the battle for India's watch market

HMT was making analogue watches, but Titan launched with the more advanced quartz technology. HMT was just a utilitarian product, enabling customers to check the time, but Titan was positioned as a fashion statement, targeting young India. They also focused on outlet locations where there was high footfall; top management themselves scouted many locations. It was also decided that Titan would deal directly with the retailers since all existing distributors were beholden to HMT. Titan would supply only against advance payment, a practice unprecedented at the time, to ensure that retailers' cash was tied up in Titan stock.

Advance payments would make for more congenial and efficient sales visits because a salesperson would not have to start the call with the unpleasant task of reminding the store owner about pending payments. In spite of initial resistance, even internally, to the idea of 'no credit to dealers', Titan put its foot down on that decision and insisted that that was the only and the best way for Titan. This was an extremely unusual policy stand and many from other industries were sure it would not work. But work it did, and in spades; in fact, it was one of the biggest contributors to Titan's initial financial success.

The seeds of the franchisee model were also sown in these early sessions. Titan proactively attracted businesspersons from outside the watch trade to set up watch shops, even if they needed extra help to do it. Partly because there were no middlemen, Titan could also offer retailers better margins. All these policies served Titan well in the initial years; they were the key to maintaining low working capital borrowings that enabled them to show profits from the very first year of operations. Fast forward to today—Titan today has sixteen brands, more than 2200 retail stores, having an area of 2.8 million square feet, and 7263 employees. Titan is the biggest wealth creator from the Tata Group, having given almost 17,000 times the returns in the last twenty years (at 2022 year-end price).[4] Starting with watches, the company successfully launched jewellery with Tanishq in 1995. It has since expanded into eyewear—Titan EyePlus, accessories and fragrance (Skinn), and its latest venture of sarees by the name of Taneira. However, among these brands, the most important to Titan's success story is Tanishq.

Tanishq

The birth of the Tanishq brand is a very interesting story. The P.V. Narasimha Rao-led government said that companies such as Titan would need to generate their own foreign exchange to fund their imports. Titan was told that the Government of India had no foreign currency to give. So they started looking for a project that could allow them to sell products overseas. In the mid-1990s, Xerxes Desai hit upon the idea of exporting jewellery for the much-needed capex. This idea was formulated when Desai visited an exhibition in Mumbai. Incidentally, the fair was called the World Watch and Jewellery Show.

Desai, Titan's first managing director, chose the name Tanishq. Tanishq derives from Ta (from Tata) and *nishq/nishk* (in Sanskrit), which means 'ornament'. However, this business also struggled for seven years. In the 1990s, Tanishq opened stores selling 18-carat jewellery, but Indians were only interested in 22-carat jewellery. The stores made losses and the stock price was left at just Rs 2. At the same time, the foray would turn out to be more difficult than anticipated, as Titan found it difficult to sway Indians from their family jewellers.

Titan's 1996–97 annual report sheds more light on this phenomenon:[5]

While Tanishq jewellery has drawn praise and evoked a very favourable reaction among consumers, the fact that our collection was initially confined to only 18 karat gold jewellery, mostly gem-set proved to be a limiting factor in the attainment of volume objectives. Work, therefore, commenced in right earnest on the creation of a new collection of 22 karat gold jewellery based on traditional Indian design themes. Tanishq's 22 karat collection has been launched recently and has evoked a most enthusiastic and, indeed, very gratifying response. While the Company believes that an 18 karat gold alloy is the most suited for jewellery—and is, in fact, the world standard for fine gold jewellery—the existence of a very strong consumer preference in India for 22 karat gold jewellery cannot be wished away. Our entry into this market segment will, it is hoped, accelerate the trend towards an official hallmarking process which will significantly benefit the consumer who, today, is often the recipient of substantially undercarataged jewellery masquerading under the 22 karat label. In addition to the introduction of 22 karat ethnic jewellery, the current financial year will see a significant increase in the number of Tanishq showrooms as new outlets are opened in Calcutta, Ahmedabad, Hyderabad, Pune and in several other towns. By the end of the financial year, Tanishq will have over 40 outlets in over 30 towns, representing India's first jewellery store chain.

Thus, in 2002–03, Tanishq started selling 22-carat jewellery and also did something very innovative that posed a very big threat to the competition. They bought a lot of karat meter machines, which cost Rs 12 lakh each. This was the first time in India where such machines could tell the purity of jewellery in terms of karats—18 or 22—and whether the gold was pure or impure. But this didn't directly convert into business. When asked the reason for this, customers replied angrily, 'You are just telling us we have impure gold, but not helping us.'

58 per cent of the jewellery that came for checking was less than 22-karat purity, so Tanishq also launched 'Impure to pure'. If the jewellery was above 19 karats, Tanishq would exchange it for 22-karat jewellery and just take making charges. This was revolutionary and it led to Tanishq finding its value proposition of purity and trust with the customers.

The commendable thing about Tanishq was that it kept innovating. Tanishq kept on launching new categories and sub-segments under categories to keep the momentum going as it had realized that the Indian market was unorganized, very large and underserved. In 2011, Titan launched Mia, a stunning range of fine urban-chic affordable jewellery crafted for working women. All the pieces in Mia were crafted in 14K gold and the collection had over 500 designs. When growth slowed between 2013 and 2016, it innovated by reducing making charges, increasing new launches backed by product innovation and offering gold exchange schemes that nudged the consumers to up-trade. Tanishq has consistently outperformed its peers.

Titan financials: the engine powering this fast car

Particulars (Rs crore)	1987–88	2021–22	CAGR (34 years)
Revenue	16.8	29,033	24.5 per cent
EBITDA	2.51	3521	23.1 per cent
Net profit	0.26	2198	25.4 per cent

Chapter 7

CRISIL

CRISIL was India's first credit rating agency. Fast forward to today, it is a 2.6-billion-dollar company that provides ratings, risk management systems, valuation frameworks and advisory services. CRISIL was among the pillars of Rakesh Jhunjhunwala's portfolio. 'One of the best stories about Rakesh is that his mother once provoked him, "You are earning so well, can't we live a bit better?" Rakesh sold some CRISIL shares and bought a large apartment in South Mumbai. He would say later, "What I sold for less than Rs 30 crore is now worth Rs 750 crore."'[1]

In India, there are a total of seven credit rating agencies (CRAs) that are allowed to give ratings to companies on the level of risk in their bonds. The ratings market is dominated by three of them, (i) CRISIL (ii) ICRA and (iii) CARE, which together cover around 95 per cent of the industry. CRISIL is the market leader. CRISIL employs more than 4000 professionals. It has offices and research centres in eleven countries including the US, the UK, Singapore, Japan and Australia. CRISIL has 3396 professionals working across their India offices with the rest abroad as per their FY21 annual report. (The FY22 annual report was yet to be published as of the date of writing this book.)

CRISIL is majority-owned by S&P Global Inc., the world's foremost provider of credit ratings, benchmarks and analytics in the global capital and commodity markets. CRISIL's clients range from micro, small and medium enterprises (MSMEs) to large corporates, investors and top global financial institutions. CRISIL works with commercial and investment banks, insurance companies, private equity players and asset management companies globally. They also work with governments and policymakers in the infrastructure space in India and other emerging markets.

CRISIL has seven broad-based product categories: ratings, SME solutions, Indian research, global research and risk solutions, global analytics, infra advisory, business intelligence and risk solutions.

CRISIL was created in January 1987. It was jointly promoted by the Housing Development Finance Corporation (HDFC), Industrial Credit and Investment Corporation of India (the erstwhile ICICI Ltd) and a few other financial institutions. There was an industry need for a business that would aid the development of a bond market in India and this was why Narayanan Vaghul and Pradip Shah, bankers from ICICI and HDFC respectively, created this institution, CRISIL, that created and pioneered an entire industry around ratings in the late 1980s and early 1990s.[2]

When CRISIL started, the concept of credit ratings was way ahead of its time. India had no such thing as a corporate bond market, its business environment wasn't really positive and lending rates were fixed. CRISIL's first client was Indian Petrochemical Corporation Limited (IPCL), which was a Rs 625 crore public-sector unit and was India's largest vertically integrated petrochemicals manufacturer.

Within two years of commencing operations, CRISIL established a who's who of a client list. It included Ashok Leyland, the Birla Group, Cholamandalam Investment and a few more well-known business names. Having an independent rating process that was influenced by CRISIL's principles and not the client's principles or vested interests had its own set of problems, however. Some clients were unhappy, some went away and some rejected their ratings. Some even tried their sources in the RBI, government institutions and other powerful institutions to try to get CRISIL to give ratings in their favour. If this was not enough, one client even threatened to destroy them. However, Mr Shah decided not to give in at any cost.

The period from 1990 to 2000 was a momentous time for CRISIL. It started off in 1990 by providing comprehensive information and analytical opinion on India's corporate entities via its 'CRISIL card service'. In 1992, thanks to CRISIL's training and technical assistance, Malaysia Berhad, a rating agency, and Maalot, the Israeli securities rating company, came into being. One very important milestone was in November 1993, when CRISIL came out with its IPO. It was a great success—its 20,00,000 shares, sold at a premium of Rs 40 per share, were oversubscribed by 2.47 times. In December 1995, it made its stock market business foray by developing and launching the CRISIL500 Equity Index. The seeds of one of the defining partnerships in credit ratings were sown in February 1996 when CRISIL forged a strategic business alliance with Standard and Poor's (S&P) Ratings Group. This was further strengthened when S&P acquired a 9.68 per cent stake in CRISIL in May 1997. CRISIL always wanted to get into non-rating businesses so that they were insulated from downcycles in the rating business. In 1996, CRISIL got into advisory services as well and got their first major order win in the infrastructure policy advisory domain. CRISIL also set up India Index Services Limited (IISL), a joint venture with the National Stock Exchange of India Limited (NSEIL), to provide indices and index-related services in Indian capital markets.

From educating companies about their products and the need for credit ratings to the CRISIL frameworks actually becoming industry-standard, life came full circle for CRISIL in 1999 when their proprietary Risk Assessment Model (RAM) became the banking industry standard.

R. Ravimohan had started his career with ICICI, where he worked on project appraisals and merchant banking, besides a host of other things. In 1994, when Pradeep Shah moved to Indocean, R. Ravimohan was elevated to MD.

In the space of the ten years that he was CEO, R. Ravimohan batted for diversification beyond the ratings businesses. He oversaw three big acquisitions, helping CRISIL transform into a ratings, research and analytics company. During his tenure of thirteen years with CRISIL, he also helped create a crucial and strategic partnership with

S&P, a leading international ratings firm, that eventually led to S&P acquiring a majority stake in CRISIL in 2005, a recognition of the significance of the Indian firm.

Interestingly, Ravimohan moved to S&P in 2007 and Roopa Kudva, a fifteen-year veteran at CRISIL who had joined in 1992 as a senior rating analyst, took over as the MD and CEO. Kudva helped the company scale up in the global arena through acquisitions in the global research and analytics business and expanded the ratings business in India by rating small and medium-sized enterprises (SMEs). CRISIL's core businesses today are ratings, global research and analytics (GR&A), India research, capital markets research and infrastructure advisory and risk solutions.

Between 2000 and 2010, CRISIL made four major acquisitions that helped them achieve explosive growth and fit right into their vision of widening their business spectrum. This decade was all about acquisitions, agility and expanding product spectrum. There was one event that changed the trajectory of this company. This was not without some failures, though.

CRISIL's first acquisition was INFAC in 2000. The acquisition was to get into industry research and outlook, something CRISIL did not have in its bouquet of products. The INFAC acquisition helped CRISIL hit two targets at once—eliminating competition and bringing in much-desired research capabilities.

CRISIL made a flawed decision and had to contend with the consequences when it launched the Healthcare Institutions Grading product in 2002. This was the culmination of a year's painstaking research and collaboration with a leading hospital chain in the country.

Ravimohan, the then CRISIL chief, embarked on a mission to bring this product to life after protracted discussions with Apollo Hospitals. The product was closed in 2007, twenty grades and five years later. The learning? Not to get into areas where they had no expertise.

CRISIL's first overseas acquisition was EconoMatters Ltd in 2003 (later the Gas Strategies Group), a London-based company providing natural gas-related consulting, information and training, and conference-organizing services. This wasn't their last overseas acquisition but one that would teach them a lot in the years to come. CRISIL had a lot of dependence on the acquired company to show synergies. To make things worse, the management team of Econo had no connect with the CRISIL team and organization. It never fit in. CRISIL divested 90 per cent of the investment in 2008 and had exited completely by 2010.

On 26 April 2005, S&P completed its acquisition of a 51 per cent stake in CRISIL. Rakesh Jhunjhunwala also tendered his shares in the open offer (when company A acquires a significant stake in company B, it is required to provide an opportunity to the existing shareholders of company B to sell their shares. This is referred to as an open offer. In India, an open offer is triggered when the acquirer buys a 25 per cent or higher stake. The acquiring company is required to make an open offer for at least 26 per cent additional shares, at a price not below the average price of the past twenty-six weeks. This provides minority shareholders an exit route in the event of a new management taking over). In a statement from New York, S&P president Kathleen A. Corbet said, 'A majority position will enable S&P to integrate CRISIL more fully into our operations for the benefit of the Indian and international marketplace.' It had been a fruitful journey between both the premier institutions till now, which was about to get even more eventful.

However, despite being acquired, CRISIL continued on its growth path and its own acquisition spree. Irevna, which was into equity research, was their second overseas acquisition in 2005 (third in the year, fourth overall). It was a leading global equity research and analytics company. Until this acquisition, CRISIL only thought about the Indian market, but this acquisition helped them step up their game and develop a global mindset.

Pipal Research, CRISIL's most recent acquisition in 2010, was a continuation of this ethos. This was to gain a foothold in the corporate business and investment research services market. This acquisition also complemented the Irevna portfolio as these two combined led to a unique product and geographical positioning: high-end analytical offshoring with the widest range of services, with leadership in the high-end global research and analytics space.

With the CRISIL engine moving forward, growing geographies and expanding business lines, its story was received well by all investors, who were happy with the company delivering good growth and being proactive. By 2011, ratings as a business was contributing only 40 per cent to CRISIL's top line, a huge change since ratings were the bread and butter for the group and the flagship business. CRISIL had come a long way and they had been successful in widening the scope of the firm's services. They were a truly diversified firm. The Irevna acquisition was a huge success, having grown manifold under the

CRISIL brand. 'Rakesh started buying CRISIL shares in 2003. After buying 10,000 shares initially at Rs 150, he later increased his holding to 5.5 million shares as of September 2006. He accumulated the CRISIL stock between Rs 400 and Rs 500. In 2013, Rekha Jhunjhunwala offloaded 4,00,000 shares for over Rs 46 crore.'[3] Currently, Rekha Jhunjhunwala and her late spouse, Rakesh, own a 5.47 per cent stake in the ratings agency, which is worth Rs 1200 crore (September 2022 shareholding data and 26 October 2022 price taken for calculation). One of the best stories about Rakesh Jhunjhunwala is that his mother once taunted him about being miserly. 'You are earning so well, can't we live a bit better?' she said. Rakesh sold some CRISIL shares in 2004–05 and bought a large apartment in South Mumbai. The CRISIL stock continued to rise. Although it is unclear exactly when in 2004–05 he sold CRISIL stock (the CRISIL stock price tripled in that year alone), by 2022, it had risen about eighteen times from its price at the end of 2005. What he sold for less than Rs 30 crore was worth Rs 1300–1500 crore at the 52-week-high price of Rs 3863.55 (that was observed on 3 May 2022) of the CRISIL stock (rough estimates).

Chapter 8

Lupin

'There is only one reason why we exist—to treat diseases, to heal and enrich human life.'

—Late Desh Bandhu Gupta

'Desh Bandhu Gupta, or DBG, as he was famously known, started Lupin in the early 1960s. Born in Rajgarh, Rajasthan, DBG completed his MSc in chemistry and started his career as a teacher at Birla Institute of Technology and Science (BITS), Pilani. He moved to Bombay in the early 1960s and started Lupin with a sum of Rs 5000, which he borrowed from his wife.'[1] The first office of Lupin was a rented premises in central Mumbai which was used for dispatching medicines. The company started with two employees. Lupin's first employees were a peon-cum-packer and a part-time typist.

Later, with a Rs 8 lakh loan from Central Bank of India, a factory was started, whose major order was to provide iron and folic acid tablets to the Government of India programmes related to mother and child healthcare. They later moved on to anti-tuberculosis (TB) drugs, which formed up to 36 per cent of the company's revenues by 2001. The company name, Lupin, is inspired by the resilient lupin flower, which grows in harsh conditions yet nourishes the soil around it. Their products range from branded and generic formulations, biotechnology products, complex generics (consumer products having no brand name or registered trademark) and APIs to over-the-counter (OTC) products and speciality pharmaceuticals that cater to the therapy protocols of tuberculosis treatment, diabetes management, central nervous system (CNS) disorders, cardiac care and respiratory disorders.[1]

At present headquartered in Mumbai, India, Lupin has a strong presence in over 100 countries, with a portfolio of more than 1000 products. It has a market capitalization of $3.8 billion and is among the top ten generic pharmaceutical companies globally. It has 457 applications for new drug approvals (ANDAs) filed with the US FDA as of March 2022, 1008 active patents, is ranked number 3 in the US by prescriptions and is number 6 in the Indian pharma market.[3]

Company's phases

Phase 1: Late 1990s to 2002, the perception of Lupin wasn't good

In 1979, the company established the first formulations facility and research and development centre in Aurangabad, India. In 1987, Lupin's cephalexin facility in

Mandideep (Madhya Pradesh) and its Ankleshwar plant went online. Afterwards, Lupin began producing anti-TB pharmaceuticals, which at one point accounted for 36 per cent of the company's revenues and made it the largest producer of TB medications in the world.[4] For a long time, Lupin mainly had one anti-TB drug, Rifampicin, a low-margin product with government controls. Lupin started out as an API player for the anti-tuberculosis segment before getting into formulations.

According to an MIT Sloan School case study (titled 'Biocon India Group', written by Archana Kalegaonkar, Richard Locke and Jonathan Lehrich dated 4 November 2008), 'starting in its earliest days, the pharma industry in India experienced phenomenal growth. A combined bulk drug and formulations output of Rs 168 crore in 1965 grew to Rs 19,737 crore thirty-five years later—an annual growth rate of 15 per cent. Roughly two-thirds of the output stayed in the domestic market which, by the year 2001, was also growing at 15 per cent annually. The remaining one-third[3]—Rs 6631 crore—went to the export market, which had a 21 per cent growth rate. By the beginning of the twenty-first century, over 20,000 pharmaceutical companies were operating in India.'

It all started with the 1972 Patent Act, when 'product patents' were disregarded. In 1970, MNCs dominated the market. The 1972 Patent Act allowed 'reverse engineering' that enabled Indian companies to reverse engineer drugs and take market share. Formulation sales in India rose from Rs 150 crore in 1965 to Rs 7935 crore in 1995. API exports started in the 1970s but really acquired pace after 1996. Bulk drugs production accelerated from Rs 18 crore in 1966 to Rs 1518 crore in 1995. India also began exporting pharmaceutical formulations to developing markets. The share of exports in total production increased from 3 per cent in 1980–81 to 24 per cent in 1994–95, with 90 per cent of exports going to developing markets.

Phase 2: 2002 to 2013—earnings recovered consistently and execution was best in class

An unrelated diversification into real estate didn't work and Lupin was saddled with bad debt (details about this are not available). 'Worse still, the stock was associated with the manipulations of tainted stockbroker Ketan Parekh. As investors clamoured for change, DBG decided to professionalize the company pretty early on and brought on board Kamal Sharma as the MD in 2003, with a mandate to reinvent and take on peers Ranbaxy and Dr Reddy's, who were expanding to new markets like the US.'[3]

In 2001, Lupin was just a Rs 280 crore market cap company with sales of Rs 900 crore. The real trigger came when governance improved. This improvement was led by Dr Kamal K. Sharma and his leadership team.

He was the one who oversaw the rise of Lupin from Rs 1120 crore business to Rs 13,702 crore (reported in fiscal 2016), with 72 per cent in revenues from its international operations in seventy-six countries.[4] He joined when the stock price of Lupin was Rs 50. At the end of FY16, the stock price was around Rs 1500.

Sharma helped Lupin diversify from being a company best known as one of the largest manufacturers of anti-TB drugs into a range of affordable generic and branded formulations in many markets. Lupin has also acquired several pharma firms across the world and Sharma has made it the first Indian company to successfully market an individual branded drug, Suprax, in the US. Former colleagues of Sharma used to say he was an expert at understanding the pharma sector. 'He used this to pull off a coup in a licensing deal while at RPG. Sharma beat a licensor down to $500,000 from $7 million it had sought.'[5]

They also moved up the value chain and mastered the business of certain intermediates and APIs. They leveraged their strengths to build a formidable formulations business. It has a significant presence in cephalosporins, cardiovasculars (prils and statins), diabetology, asthma and the non-steroidal anti-inflammatory drugs (NSAIDs) therapy segments.[6]

> At the start of the new century, Lupin made some bold moves, which accelerated revenue growth and propelled the company into a different orbit over the next ten years: (a) entry into the US market—transition from low-cost to branded generics in the US when no other Indian manufacturer had been able to establish a meaningful presence in the category; (b) change in the India business strategy—a focus shift from acute to chronic therapies and formulations for APIs; (c) entry into Japan—Lupin became the first international generics company to gain a foothold in Japan. The above efforts resulted in 23 per cent revenue CAGR from FY04 to FY17.[7]

Lupin grew faster than the industry at 20 per cent CAGR from FY01 to FY17. The industry grew at 17 per cent during these fifteen years.

2014–21—Massive blunders in capital allocations and misgovernance, non-compliance . . . perfect storm of negatives

In 2015, the Lupin share price had reached almost Rs 2000 at its peak, but then many US FDA issues cropped up, not just for Lupin but for many Indian listed pharma players. In 2015–16, pharma companies' Indian facilities were issued twenty warning letters as per Lupin's September 2017 presentation. Data integrity was the biggest cause of the warning letters in these two years. But there were also other compliance issues—procedures not being followed, scientifically unsound laboratory controls and investigation of discrepancies and failures. This cast a very big shadow on the compliance levels of Indian pharma companies as critical functions were not being followed properly.

'Around 2015–16, Lupin started facing increased problems in its US business due to increased generic competition, generic price erosion and customer consolidation. This was accentuated by a spate of US FDA observations, impacting the company's financial performance in the last few years.'[8] US generics revenue became subdued from FY15 onwards. Operating profit/ EBITDA margins also reduced with the decline in US revenue after FY15.

Due to the business environment worsening, the company's return efficiency ratios also started falling. The return on capital employed, which is used to assess a company's profitability and capital efficiency, declined for Lupin and the industry as a whole. This ratio helps us understand how well a company is generating profits from its capital. The working capital cycle was also stretched.

The Working Capital Cycle (WCC) is the time it takes to convert raw material into actual revenue inflows. A long cycle (a greater number of days) means more time taken to earn revenue and a greater number of the days the raw material is being stuck in a process. Short cycles (a smaller number of days) mean quicker conversion into revenue that allows a business free cash to redeploy it again for other purposes, which leads to agility. The WCC for Lupin was elongated/stretched as receivables (money they were supposed to receive) surged after consolidation in the US market. There was also a continuous build-up of inventories (meaning raw material was stuck on the company's balance sheet) in US subsidiaries.

In July 2015, the company announced its intention to acquire Gavis Pharmaceuticals and Novel Laboratories for $880 million. When it comes to US FDA compliances, Lupin went from having one of the best track records (till 2015–16) among its peers, to an average or subpar track record as of today.

To put this in perspective, a few of their key plants got US FDA observations one after the other. And not just that, there were repeat observations at the Goa facility (in fact, there was a total of seven observations during re-inspection, which showed a lax compliance approach in the company given how they were inspected before also) in September 2021. At present, five sites of Lupin either have warning letters of Official Action Indicated (OAI) status from the US Food and Drug Administration.

The company's Goa plant was inspected in March 2017 and subsequently, the company received a warning letter for the facility. The plant was again re-inspected at the beginning of 2019, and the FDA had then issued a 'Form 483' with two or more observations.[9]

In September 2017, the company, in its quarterly earnings release, talked about how the current model of Indian pharma was ageing. In the US, pricing pressure was visible and the space was becoming hyper-competitive.[10] In FY17, Lupin's raw material cost, employee cost and other expenses as a percentage of sales were 28.6 per cent, 16.3 per cent and 29.4 per cent, respectively. These costs added up to a total of 74.3 per cent of sales, which in FY22 rose to a total of 86.8 per cent.[11]

Its gross margins (that show how well the company is managing its raw material costs), at 67.4 per cent in FY15, fell to 60.5 per cent in FY22. Return on equity (ROE) is a gauge of a corporation's profitability and how efficiently it generates those profits. The higher the ROE, the better a company is at converting its equity financing into profits. For Lupin, the ROE was 30.4 per cent in FY15, which fell to just 2 per cent in FY22—again one of the highest falls in the industry. In March 2019, the US FDA put several Lupin drug plants on notice for quality problems, and indicated that it might not approve future Lupin drug applications.

In November 2019, Lupin made a provision of US$ 53.5 million (Rs 380 crore) to be paid towards the settlement amount in respect of a State of Texas lawsuit in the US against Lupin for reporting inflated drug prices to the Medicaid programme. If that wasn't enough, Gavis, the very famous acquisition, started showing cracks. Lupin made a lot of impairments after the acquisition of Gavis, which dented many quarters' net profits. The company had to incur its first impairment on assets of Gavis Pharma in

January–March 2018, and the second impairment was in December 2019, when it made a Rs 1580 crore impairment. 'I would say that it (the write-offs) is done, and what we have left on the books in terms of intangible assets is $100 million, which is also supported by the business we have in place,'[12] chief executive officer Vinita Gupta said in a call with journalists (the October–December 2019 quarter con-call). 'Lupin posted a net loss of Rs 511.9 crore for the fourth quarter of fiscal 2021–22 due to rising costs, price erosion in the US and impairment expenses of Rs 126.7 crore for US-based Gavis.'[13]

As we can tell from many of the events recounted above, this phase was a very tumultuous one for Lupin, with bad capital allocations and a few losses. Adjusted earnings per share growth rate for FY18–22 for Lupin was -33 per cent. Operating to free cash flow conversion was just 11 per cent for Lupin during FY13–22, which was the lowest among peers. This showed that the company had very weak surplus generation capability. Now this is important, as free cash flow helps the company fund future projects or R&D projects or, say, buybacks with their own internal surplus and not rely on external debt or equity raising, which can be very costly. In Q1FY23, it reported its lowest quarterly EBITDA margin of 4.5 per cent due to restructuring in the US as well as continuous inflation of raw materials and freight.[14] The US revenue stood at a multi-year low as well.

If we look at recent times, there are some early signs of course correction but, more importantly, valuations are indeed compensating for past mistakes. The company's story has many moving blocks.

Rakesh Jhunjhunwala's tryst with Lupin

Rakesh started buying Lupin shares in 2003 when the market cap was around Rs 500 crore (Rs 147–699 range). In June 2007, he held a 3.45 per cent stake in Lupin. However, thereafter, Rakesh reduced the stake gradually and exited the company fully in September 2021, when the market capitalization was around Rs 44,000 crore. It can be definitely termed as a good exit as the year 2021 saw minus 5 per cent returns for the calendar year and perhaps that's what led to the Big Bull exiting. One must also note that from 3.65 per cent in June 2010 to 1.6 per cent in June 2021, and finally to less than 1 per cent in September 2021— the Big Bull was continuously trimming the position, despite its substantial wealth creation for him in the early years.

Annexure for shareholding reduction in Lupin by RJ:
June 2007 – 3.45 per cent
June 2008 – 3.36 per cent
June 2009 – 3.63 per cent
June 2010 – 3.65 per cent
June 2011 – 1.73 per cent
June 2012 – 1.87 per cent
June 2013 – 2.09 per cent
June 2014 – 1.57 per cent
June 2015 – 1.45 per cent
June 2018 – 1.95 per cent
June 2020 – 1.47 per cent
September 2020 – 1.53 per cent
December 2020 – 1.6 per cent
March 2021 – 1.6 per cent
June 2021 – 1.6 per cent
September 2021 – Less than 1 per cent

Chapter 9

DHFL

Roti, kapda, makaan (food, clothing, shelter)—the three basic needs of every person.

In the Indian context, owning one's own makaan or house is definitely an indicator of economic well-being. Helping folks achieve this dream was indeed one of the reasons that DHFL came into existence.

The late Shri Rajesh Kumar Wadhawan, promoter, Dewan Housing Finance Corporation Limited (DHFL), was convinced that no country could expect to progress sustainably if a large proportion of its population continued to be financially excluded. The result was DHFL, which entered the Indian housing finance industry in 1984 and became an early player in the segment.

The company definitely did very well for the next twenty-seven to thirty years. Its revenues increased from Rs 103 crore in 2001 to Rs 10,464 crore in 2018, a CAGR of 31.2 per cent, and increased its net profit from Rs 16 crore in 2001 to Rs 2900 crore in 2017, clocking a CAGR of 38.4 per cent. Loan disbursements were Rs 161 crore in 2001, which increased to Rs 44,800 crore in 2018, clocking a 39.3 per cent CAGR.[1]

India's housing finance industry crossed the Rs 7 trillion/Rs 7 lakh crore mark in December 2012 and was predicted to maintain a healthy annual growth of between 17 and 19 per cent. Yet, the country remained extensively underpenetrated when it came to housing finance. Mortgage finance stood at 9 per cent of GDP as compared to Asian peers, such as China at 20 per cent, Korea at 26 per cent, and western economies such as the US at 80 per cent and the UK at 83 per cent.[2]

> Brothers Kapil and Dheeraj Wadhawan, the promoters of DHFL, were the toast of the Mumbai corporate circuit. Kapil joined in 1997 and together with Dheeraj, oversaw a turnaround in the fortunes and trajectory of the company. The brothers also expanded the business through a string of acquisitions and diversified it from a pure home loan company to a broader financial services firm that extended loans for education and to small and medium enterprises, and entered the life and general life insurance business, besides mutual funds. They also lived life king-size, owning a private plane, a yacht and a fleet of luxury cars, including a Rolls-Royce Phantom and a Bentley, and moved around with gun-toting bodyguards.[3]

All was going well, but the company started facing problems after FY17–18.

Particulars/ year (Rs cr.)	FY16–17	FY17–18	FY18–19	FY19–20
Revenue	8857.2	10,464.5	12,902.5	9578.9
PAT (profit after tax)	2896.5	1172.1	–1036.1	–13,426.85
Deposits with DHFL	6769	9652	6588	5728.89
GNPA	0.94 per cent	0.96 per cent	2.72 per cent	62.97 per cent

'Only when the tide goes out do you discover who's been swimming naked.'

—Warren Buffett

After Infrastructure Leasing & Financial Services Ltd (IL&FS), a systemically important non-deposit-accepting core investment company, started defaulting on various payments (including bank loan repayments and commercial paper [CP] redemption obligations) beginning August 2018, there was a cascading effect on the whole financial sector in an adverse way.

Subsequently, the credit rating agencies ICRA, CARE and Brickwork abruptly downgraded IL&FS and its subsidiaries from high investment grade to junk status. This event sent shockwaves across the country's shadow lending, that is, the non-banking financial companies (NBFC) sector. Creditors, mostly scheduled commercial banks (SCBs), rushed to tighten lending norms against NBFCs. This sparked a brutal liquidity crisis that affected all NBFCs, big and small. One of those was DHFL.

Since 2016, IL&FS had been relying mainly on short-term loans for its funding requirements. But it extended long-term loans to infrastructure projects. This led to an asset-liability mismatch. Short-term liabilities were used to finance long-term assets. This made the company vulnerable to a liquidity crisis as its assets generated returns only in the long term.

In September 2018, DSP Mutual Funds sold over Rs 300 crore worth of commercial papers of DHFL at a discount. This is because DHFL had major exposure to IL&FS. It had lent Rs 649 crore to IL&FS.

Later, DHFL chairman Kapil Wadhawan clarified: 'The stock fell due to unfortunate panic in the system following rumours of a liquidity crisis. Liquidity is not an issue. We have liquidity of Rs 10,000 crore and we do not carry too many CPs in our books. . . DHFL has neither defaulted on any bonds or repayment, nor has there been any single instance of a delay on any of its repayment liabilities. We do not have any exposure with IL&FS.'[4]

The DHFL share price fell 59.67 per cent intraday or 364 points to a new low of 246.25, the sharpest fall among the NBFCs, on 21 September 2018. It lost nearly Rs 8129 crore in market capitalization on the same day.

After the IL&FS crisis, banks became wary of lending to the NBFCs, which impacted DHFL. It had trouble raising further loans from the financial market. This problem was compounded due to an asset-liability mismatch on the balance sheets of NBFCs. Simply put, short-term liabilities were used to finance long-term assets. In other words, DHFL relied on short-term loans from banks to give out loans to home buyers. These short-term loans from banks dried up after the IL&FS crisis. DHFL's finances, too, suffered as a result of declining investments and rising demands to meet its obligations. Essentially, since September 2017, DHFL had been playing catch up on its financial obligations—that too without fresh money to count on and a worsening loans portfolio. GST, RERA and demonetization had further compounded its problems as many fly-by-night operators/builders suddenly saw their businesses go under. This further dented DHFL's balance sheet and profits as DHFL was known to lend money to such entities.

The FY18–19 annual report states: DHFL was at its peak in September 2018, originating close to Rs 2000 crore of retail loans per month, when the liquidity crisis hit the NBFC sector. DHFL had to stop all new origination and adopt caution to conserve liquidity to meet all financial obligations and service all partially disbursed cases for balance requirements. With no fresh inflow of resources, the company opted for securitization of its assets as the single source of funds for meeting all obligations on time. In the six months leading to the end of the fiscal in March 2019, they monetized assets valued at over Rs 15,630 crore and repaid over Rs 22,700 crore of liabilities. Securitization is the selling of loans to a third party.[5]

On 29 January 2019, something very unexpected happened that definitely shocked everyone to the core. Cobrapost, a Indian news site that is known for its undercover investigative journalism, made some allegations about DHFL. It said:

> 'In what appears to be the biggest banking scam in Indian history, the primary promoters of DHFL have been found to have siphoned off more than Rs. 31,000 crore of public money. The scam has primarily been pulled off through grants of loans and advances to shell companies and by using other means. Money has also been routed through these dubious companies and parked outside India, to acquire assets. Cobrapost has unearthed the scam by closely analyzing documents available with public authorities and information available in public domain.'[6]

Then, on 4 June 2019, the inevitable happened. DHFL defaulted on Rs 900 crore ($122.6 million) worth of due payments. Its CPs' rating was downgraded to 'D' overnight, which sent its share price into a tailspin. Cases were filed against DHFL by depositors.

To add to DHFL's woes, allegations of dubious financial transactions continued to emerge against Kapil Wadhawan (the then chairman and MD) and Dheeraj Wadhawan (then a non-executive director). Finally, on 29 November 2019, the RBI initiated insolvency proceedings against DHFL—the first NBFC to undergo a corporate insolvency resolution process (CIRP). The Union Bank of India alleged that Kapil and Dheeraj Wadhawan, in criminal conspiracy with others, misrepresented and concealed facts, committed criminal breach of trust and abused public funds to cheat the consortium to the tune of Rs 34,614 crore by defaulting on loan repayments from May 2019 onwards.

To add to that, the agency also unearthed a scam linked to the Pradhan Mantri Awas Yojana (PMAY). According to the CBI, Kapil and Dheeraj Wadhawan created 'fake and fictitious' home loan accounts amounting to over Rs 14,000 crore and availed Rs 1880 crore in interest subsidy from the Government of India. Later, 'the CBI booked DHFL directors Kapil Wadhawan, Dheeraj Wadhawan and others for allegedly defrauding seventeen banks of Rs 34,615 crore. This is the biggest case of bank fraud ever registered by the CBI.'[7] Only ABG Shipyard comes close—it was booked for defrauding banks of Rs 23,000 crore. If that wasn't enough, the CBI accused the Wadhawan brothers of giving loans to their owned companies/developers fraudulently, while the records show that the loans were given to retail/individual borrowers, who in fact did not exist.

The Bandra Books of Kapil Wadhawan

A scheme called 'Bandra Books' was created to carry out this scam. DHFL set up a dummy branch that existed only in theory, or virtually. A bifurcation was made in the internal loan management software and they showed their auditors that they distributed home loans worth Rs 2.6 lakh crore to individuals. But in reality, they disbursed an amount of Rs 11,000 crore to ninety-one companies that were owned by themselves. As one would have guessed, this was a front for money routing. The money flowed into the promoters' own companies. CBI found out in the investigation that the promoters enjoyed this money by spending it on expensive art, cars and luxury properties. Even worse, some of this money allegedly found its way into the underworld, to dreaded gangster Chhota Shakeel.

There were allegations against DHFL that it had created dummy loans and hence, their books of accounts were all untrue. There were also reports allegedly suggesting that if DHFL hadn't made these fictitious entries to their promoter group and not lent to promoter entities through a maze of transactions, it would have shown a loss for ten out of the last eleven years.

(The text above has been taken from the DHFL Auditor's report.)

To sum it up, here's a list of things that were allegedly done by DHFL to orchestrate this grand scam.

Loans to shell companies: A shell corporation refers to a dummy company whose existence is confined to documents and it has no physical presence, no office, no employees. It has no active business operations running, with no tangible assets or plat, property or equipment in its possession. But it is used to hide a person's or another company's activities, sometimes illegal ones. The scrutiny of account books showed that sixty-six entities having commonalities with DHFL promoters were disbursed Rs 29,100 crore, against which Rs 29,849 crore remained outstanding.[8]

Round tripping: Round tripping is an illegal way to inflate revenues by passing on assets to other promoter firms usually on a no-profit basis to show growth and then buying them back later. It results in no economic benefit; it is merely a series of transactions to artificially depict growth.

Purchasing assets: The last step of this scam was, of course, purchasing assets for personal gains. Assets were purchased in other countries. The list contained properties in Mauritius, Dubai, a cricket team in the Sri Lankan Premier League and some start-up companies in the UK.

What were the red flags?

DHFL's large lending was to developers. The prolonged real-estate slowdown should have made them more cautious. There was an asset-liability mismatch. DHFL, an NBFC, believed that they would be able to roll over their short-term borrowings without any problems till eternity. But the IL&FS episode led to liquidity tightening in the economy. A small hole can sink a great ship.

Big Bull checks in

In 2013, Rakesh bought 25 lakh shares of DHFL at Rs 135 a share for Rs 34 crore. As of September 2012, DHFL looked interesting. They had a portfolio approach to lending, where different subsidiaries catered to different customer niches differentiated by the price of the dwelling unit. DHFL concentrated on Tier II and III areas where the competition was not that intense. They had a pan-India presence. It was a dominant player in the low- and middle-income group. It also had tie-ups with various banks like Yes Bank, UBI, CBI and Punjab and Sind Bank. It also cross-sold insurance to its customers, besides offering technical consultancy and management to developers and self-construction clients in Tier II and Tier III locations.

> In a moment of candour, Rakesh revealed during a chat with Ramesh Damani and N. Jayakumar that he bought DHFL without doing any research and only because it was quoting at a rock-bottom valuation, offered a high dividend yield and had been growing consistently at 20 per cent for the past ten years. 'Such ridiculous valuations! . . . What is there to think? So these kinds of situations are like invest now, investigate later,' the Badshah is said to have exclaimed. 'Today, it is like meeting Aishwarya Rai—what are you thinking? You date her without thinking,' he added, much to the amusement of Ramesh Damani and N. Jayakumar.[9]

In a video interview, he said, 'I met Mr Wadhawan two times, once on a flight and once he came to office.' Rakesh bought fifty lakh shares in four days without any research. 'What is the need? The opportunity size is alluring. He is the largest disburser of housing loans below Rs 12.5 lakh in India. The book will be Rs 40,000 crore this year. The loan to housing sector is going to be one of the biggest areas in the financial business; look at the opportunity size. IFC invested with him. His father was a visionary who set this up in 1984 for houses below Rs 5 lakh. Sundaram commands higher PE as it has a niche; this fellow also has a niche,' he said in a 2013 interview. He further added, 'He has a dream, vision, sensibility. The stock trades at 0.5 times the book value, three times earnings and at a 4 per cent yield. One day it will be one to two times the book value. He's growing at 20 per cent every year, think of it. Today, it is 2013; at the end of 2016, it will be Rs 800 stock at 1.5 times the price to book value.'[10]

Rakesh held 1,00,00,000 shares (post-bonus) of DHFL. The holding was worth Rs 202 crore.[11] Perhaps this was one of the biggest miscalculations of Rakesh's investing career—he should have delved deeper. It's worth noting that even in the case of Titan, he bought a block from a broker and then met the management, after which he was convinced and he bought more shares. Fast forward to 2018—DHFL found itself crumbling after the IL&FS issue sent shockwaves across the money markets, with stronger ones through the ecosystem companies. However, after this, Rakesh bought more on this bet, buying another 0.43 per cent stake. Rakesh said that 'he sees a bigger picture. To your surprise, when DHFL tumbles, it is actually creating a buying opportunity because many analysts see this stock performing well in coming months too.'[12]

Big Bull Rakesh Jhunjhunwala bought 13.34 lakh shares of DHFL in what was the worst quarter for the stock in its trading history. The ace investor raised his stake in the housing finance company by 39 basis points to take his holding to 3.19 per cent at the end of the September 2018 quarter, from 2.8 per cent at the end of the June 2018 quarter. Earlier, during Diwali in November 2018, Rakesh had given an interview. When asked about NBFCs' liquidity concerns, he showed full faith in the sector and also said that it would not tumble below the level it had seen earlier. He also mentioned that the housing finance sector was the need of the hour for economic growth.[13]

The quantum of loss in DHFL was such that the company, which was trading at near Rs 650 levels in the first two weeks in September, crumbled quickly to an all-time low of Rs 179.05 per piece on 25 October 2018. Following this, Rakesh reduced his holding to 2.46 per cent, offloading 0.73 per cent or 77,28,500 shares. After this, there were many audits and investigations, many events unfolded and finally, DHFL ceased to be an entity. Piramal bought some parts of the company.

DHFL: The final chapter

DHFL, with an outstanding debt of over Rs 90,000 crore, was acquired by the Piramal group for Rs 34,250 crore. It formally acquired the bankrupt DHFL by making a cash payment of Rs 14,700 crore to creditors as per the resolution plan and issuance of debt instruments of Rs 19,550 crore (ten-year NCDs at 6.75 per cent p.a. on a half-yearly basis).

'The Piramal group's proposal to delist DHFL was accepted by DHFL's creditors in January 2021. Unaware of this, many investors continued to buy DHFL shares, anticipating a turnaround under its new owners. The number of the retail shareholders of DHFL rose from 3,16,000 in December 2020 to 3,25,000 in March 2021. On 14 June, shares of DHFL stopped trading on the exchanges, which informed investors that the resolution plan provided for their delisting.'[14]

Chapter 10

A2Z Infra

A2Z Infra (earlier A2Z Maintenance and Engineering Services), launched in January 2002, was an unlisted pick for Rakesh Jhunjhunwala. He bought about 21 per cent stake in the company in 2006 for around Rs 15 crore (Rakesh is said to have paid a per share price of below Rs 14). He decided to make a partial exit when the company's IPO was launched in 2010. However, it listed on a discount to its issue price. He stayed invested in the company for the next couple of years until he realized the error in his judgement. Rakesh sold his stake in the company in January 2015. He had already reduced his stake in the previous years. January 2015 was the first time his name stopped appearing in the company's shareholding pattern report. It suggests that an investor has either reduced their stake below 1 per cent or sold it off. Notably, a company must disclose the identity of all shareholders who hold more than 1 per cent of its shares. A great judge of character and promoter's potential,

Rakesh nevertheless made one of his prominent mistakes in A2Z Infrastructure.

The background

Amit Mittal acquired the equity shares of A2Z Maintenance from its existing shareholders between December 2003 and February 2004. The company was initially engaged in the Facility Management System (FMS) business and entered the Engineering, Procurement and Construction (EPC) business in fiscal 2006. FMS can be defined as the tools and services that support the functionality, safety and sustainability of buildings, grounds, infrastructure and real estate. As an EPC player, with a special focus on the distribution segment, A2Z had been providing services to the power transmission and distribution sectors. EPC firms deliver a complete package of resources to complete infrastructure projects. EPC services typically provide a single responsible source for executing a project, thus alleviating risk for the owner. The company was also into renewable energy, providing municipal solid waste management services and even IT solutions to power utilities.

A2Z carried out a lot of action on the merger and acquisition side to grow themselves. To further strengthen their presence in the EPC business, the company acquired Sri Eswara Sai Constructions Private Limited, a company engaged in the installation of transmission lines, and merged it into the company in January 2008.

To streamline operations and enhance their business focus, they transferred their FMS business to their wholly-owned subsidiary, A2Z Infraservices, in April 2008.

They increased their presence in the FMS segment in August 2009 via the acquisition of Imatek, a company that initially held a 5 per cent equity interest in CNCS (an FMS company). Imatek subsequently increased its equity interest in CNCS to 51 per cent in October 2009.

In Q1 of fiscal year 2011, they entered into agreements to purchase Surindar Chowdhury and Brothers, a partnership firm that was engaged in the business of construction of electrical substations and railway electrification work; Mohd Rashid Contractor, a partnership firm engaged in the business of telecommunications and other EPC services; and En-Tech Engineers and Contractors, a partnership firm engaged in the business of telecommunications and other EPC services. They were also expected to ramp up their holding to 51 per cent from 1 per cent in Star Transformers, a partnership firm, engaged in the business of manufacturing and fabrication of transformers.

The IPO

A2Z's main business was installation of power distribution lines and substations. The company, which started off with the not very glorious nor unique business model of maintenance work, got its big business break with the PSU Power Grid. Its big investment break came thanks to Rakesh Jhunjhunwala. This became the company's speciality, since he had picked up 21 per cent stake in the company before they launched their IPO. He had bought the stake in 2006 for around Rs 15 crore. With the company going public, he planned to take some money off the table.

Even as the market was going nowhere, A2Z Maintenance decided to come out with an IPO. The IPO was open from 8 to 10 December 2010. The issue size was Rs 675 crore. In the run-up to the IPO, the company's financials were stellar. Revenue was Rs 181 crore in FY07, which rose to Rs 1225 crore in FY10, an amazing CAGR of 89 per cent. Net profit was Rs 11.1 crore in FY07, which rose to Rs 99 crore in FY10, an amazing CAGR of 107 per cent. But during the same period, EBITDA margins had not grown much, and margins were likely to be pressured going forward, considering the growth plateau expected in the Indian EPC sector in the coming years.[1]

Disregarding the advice of close friends, Rakesh pushed the management to go ahead with the IPO in a weak market, and even leaned on some of his friends and associates to ensure that the issue was fully subscribed.

Objectives of the IPO

To get better margins and build a stronger and more marketable business model, 'A2Z diversified into other innovative industries such as managing municipal solid waste, and later into small-scale power generation activities using biomass. It was also an early entrant into the business of reducing transmission and distribution losses, where it was a partner of Sterlite Technologies. But apart from the EPC business, most of the later diversifications are yet to contribute much to the top line yet.'[2]

Through the IPO, A2Z wanted to raise Rs 675 crore through the issue of fresh shares (meaning the company gets the money). But some of the existing investors—the Big Bull included—were looking to divest a part of their stake through the IPO hence the total issue size was about Rs 860 crore, with the price band being Rs 400–410 a share.

At that price, Rakesh's stake in the company was valued at Rs 492 crore—a return of ~25–33 times in less than five years when compared to the Rs 15–20 crore invested in the business in 2006. He had offered 10 lakh shares in the IPO, enough to recoup his initial investment, and would still be left with plenty. He would get Rs 41 crore from this sale, enough to cover his initial cost of acquisition and leave surplus as well. As of the draft red herring prospectus (DRHP) filing date, Jhunjhunwala held 1.20 crore shares in the company, which were worth Rs 492 crore.

The company raised Rs 125 crore by placing a portion of the issue with anchor investors (anchor investors are institutions that are allotted shares at a fixed price before the IPO opens to the public. Each investor is required to invest at least Rs 10 crore and the funds are subject to a thirty-day lock-in period. Investment by anchor investors ahead of the IPO creates a buzz among retail investors) at Rs 400 a share. But other institutional investors did not show the same enthusiasm, as they felt the issue was overpriced. Even high-net-worth individuals (HNIs) were not excited about the issue. The institutional and retail portions of the book were undersubscribed, while the non-institutional portion was subscribed 3.12 times, helping make up the shortfall and helping the IPO sail through.

As expected, the shares had a very bad listing. They opened at a discount, never to go back above the issue price. The Big Bull bought 13.7 lakh shares worth Rs 48 crore at around Rs 350 per share and even the promoter, Amit Mittal, bought 9 lakh shares at around the same price. They thought their purchase would attract fresh buyers and stop the stock's fall, but their purchases ended up only providing an exit to the investors looking to run away from the stock. The stock finished the first day of its listing at Rs 329, a good 18 per cent below the issue price.

FY11 was good for the company. That year, India faced an energy shortage of approximately 10.10 per cent of total energy requirements and 12.70 per cent of peak demand requirements.[3] The company talked about how its execution and the governmental push and reforms in the power sector posed a great opportunity for them. The consolidated net worth of the company increased from Rs 421 crore in FY10 to Rs 1152 crore in FY11. The management talked about how their expertise and experience in FMS and EPC services was helping them expand into the areas of clean and green energy with annuity revenue streams and transforming into a complete infrastructure services company. FY12 and FY13 still turned out to be bad years. The company made a loss of Rs 18 crore in FY12 versus a profit of Rs 77 crore the previous year. Revenue fell to Rs 939 crore, and losses increased to Rs 106 crore by FY13. The debt mounted as well.

Rakesh may have sensed impending misfortunes. He resigned from the board of A2Z in October 2012 and started reducing his stake but did not give up on the company yet. The promoters, who held 44.68 per cent stake in the company as of 31 December 2012, pledged 45 per cent of it as per the BSE shareholding pattern.

FY14 was when the dominoes started falling and the stock started nosediving. The Indian economy was in the doldrums. The GDP growth rate slipped to 5 per cent in FY13, the lowest in the previous decade. With the economy stressed, infrastructure, construction and allied sectors bore most of the toll. The company said that as a result of this, 'they did not pick up any new EPC order between FY2011–12 and FY2013–14 and rather focused on delivering on-going projects'.[4]

The annual report also mentioned how the auditors were saying that the company was facing liquidity problems and that there were doubts about the company being a going concern. The company had incurred a net loss of Rs 194 crore. There was the situation relating to the corporate debt restructuring scheme as well. There was a loss of Rs 6 crore as well due to thefts of material at site (Rs 1.3 crore was recovered through insurance).

A2Z Maintenance and Engineering Services Ltd changed its company name to A2Z Infra Engineering Ltd from 31 December 2014 onwards.

Jhunjhunwala had had enough by then. He sold all his shares by January 2015, going by the shareholding pattern report. FY15 was again a bad report, where it talked about how Rs 200 crore of excess revenue was recognized in previous years. The company piled on its losses in FY16 and FY17 despite making efforts. In FY16, they added some end-consumer-facing retail products and Magic Genie Home Services for facility, maintenance and repair services for individual households. In FY17, they talked about their global expansion in Nepal and Tanzania in addition to other African countries. But nothing helped.

Fast forward to FY22, revenue was at Rs 353 crore, a fourth of what it was in FY11. Losses were at Rs 179 crore, down from its peak of Rs 433 crore in FY16, but the net worth stood at Rs 159 crore, a tenth of what it was in FY11.

What went wrong

A2Z, being an EPC player, was involved in the government-controlled power sector. They were dependent on state power utilities for their payments, which were themselves financially weak to begin with. Needless to say, there were delays in payments. The company made all expenses upfront and even took on debt. Its fixed, variable and interest costs were continuously running without any inflows. On top of it, the company had acquired a lot of other companies. It ventured out into too many businesses with the government where the cash flows (revenue inflows or payment by the government for their contracts) were very late. Time ran out for A2Z, which faced severe liquidity issues and defaulted on their debt obligations.

The CEO of RARE Enterprises, Utpal Sheth, later explained that poor capital allocation and poor capital structure created a vicious circle, which led to the doom of these companies. The return on capital employed being generated out of the business was poor and so, though there was growth, the free cash flow generation and ROCE was poor. 'Return on capital employed and scalability are two big mantras for long-term valuation creation for the company and wealth creation for the investors,' Utpal Sheth said.[5]

Rakesh and A2Z Infra

As of December 2010, Rakesh and his wife together held 19.11 per cent in the company. They maintained this stake till March 2012. In June 2012, they together held 22.68 per cent. This was maintained till September 2012 but in December 2012, it was reduced to 19.92 per cent.

Particulars

(Rs Cr)—Consolidated	2010–11	2011–12	2012–13	2013–14	2014–15	2015–16	2016–17	2021–22
Revenue	1359	1363	939	699	594	1349	995	353
Net profit	79.4	–17.6	–106	–94	–299	–433	–305	–179
Net Worth	1152	1109	1004	759	565	485	359	159
Finance Costs	62	75	107	121	170	188	200	28
Debt	317	594	679	836	820	832	816	385

March 2013—18.03 per cent

September 2013—16.7 per cent

December 2013—10 per cent. This was maintained till March 2014. In June 2014, Rakesh held only 4.04 per cent.

December 2014—3.47 per cent

January 2015—His name and his wife's name were no longer among the company's named shareholders, which meant he had exited the company fully or trimmed his stake below 1 per cent.

A2Z had a bad debut on the stock markets despite the Jhunjhunwala name being associated with it, and the company's stock sadly went on to join the ranks of penny stocks as of today.

The stock trades at Rs 11.50 as of 4 November 2022.

A2Z wasn't a pleasant experience for Jhunjhunwala. Some people talk about the promoter duping or lying to Rakesh, which he failed to catch. He was humble enough to cut his positions gradually and make a graceful exit.

Chapter 11

Mandhana Retail Ventures

'Wear clothes that matter' is a very famous quote when we talk about dressing well. Perhaps Rakesh Jhunjhunwala took this policy a notch higher and decided to invest in a company that made clothes that mattered. This was Mandhana Retail Ventures.

Before we talk about Mandhana Retail Ventures, where the Big Bull invested, we have to understand Mandhana Industries. This is because Mandhana Retail Ventures had been demerged from this company. Rakesh had invested in Mandhana Retail Ventures in 2016 after the demerger was concluded. Besides Rakesh, it was the Salman Khan connection that would keep the company in the limelight.

It was Mandhana Industries that originally had the rights to manufacture, retail and distribute the brand products of Being Human, a brand that Bollywood actor Salman Khan owns. Being Human operated as a retail division of Mandhana Industries between 2012 and 2016. 'The board of directors of Mandhana Industries, on 22 November 2014, had approved the demerger of the company's retail and trading business under the brand Being Human to Mandhana Retail Ventures Limited (MRVL). Shareholders of Mandhana Industries received two equity shares of MRVL for every three Mandhana Industries shares held. It was 14 December 2016 when the demerger finally happened.'[1]

The sole rights of the brand Being Human went to MRVL post-demerger.

Being Human is a clothing brand that sells T-shirts, shirts and lowers for men and tops and leggings for women. They also launched accessories along the way, including caps, wallets and belts. Actor Salman Khan started 'Being Human, The Salman Khan Foundation'. The foundation is structured as a charitable trust to empower the underprivileged and underserved through education and healthcare initiatives.

Mandhana Industries was incorporated as Mandhana Textile Mills Private Limited, a textile trading company, on 25 July 1984 by Purushottam Mandhana. Production and processing activities started in 1994. After fabrics processing, they got into international garments by exporting to European markets in 1998. Gradually, they expanded across cities in India, from Delhi and Chennai to Bengaluru.

In 2010, the company launched an IPO to raise Rs 107.90 crore, where it got Rs 15 crore from anchor investors. The company then established a garment unit in 2013 in Tarapur with a capacity of 20,00,000 pieces annually and another in Baramati with a capacity of producing 20,00,000 pieces annually.

January 2013 was when they inked an exclusive agreement with Being Human. With this agreement, Mandhana got exclusive marketing, designing and distribution rights for the brand for the next nine years and three months. This was an important deal as Being Human played on three key aspects that worked for its strong brand recall. The three attributes were that 1) the sales of Being Human went to charitable causes so the brand stood for something larger than just clothes and people took pride in wearing the brand, 2) designs and quality came at good prices, which worked very well for a price-conscious market like India, and 3) the association and branding/marketing by Salman Khan made it an aspirational brand for viewers and fans.

In FY16, a year before the demerger, 'Mandhana Industries Limited was a multi-division, multi-geography company. It was one of India's leading textile and garment manufacturers. The company manufactured products at its state-of-the-art facilities and exported to twenty-five countries. Vertical integration enabled the company to span the entire textile value chain, enhancing growth opportunities.'[2]

Over eleven years, from 2005 to 2016, the company's financials had done very well. From Rs 127 crore in FY05 and Rs 463 crore in FY09 to Rs 1646 crore in FY16, revenue grew at a CAGR of 26.23 per cent. Net profit had increased from a mere Rs 6.4 crore in FY05 to Rs 37 crore in FY09 to Rs 57 crore in FY16, clocking a CAGR of 22 per cent. Exports had grown from Rs 47 crore in FY05 to Rs 136 crore in FY09 to Rs 238 crore in FY16. Debt-to-equity in 2016 had expanded to 1.5 times and this would come to trouble them later, as we will see. In fact, in 2016, their net profit went down to Rs 58 crore, from Rs 64 crore in 2015, due to an increase in interest costs.[3]

The post-demerger story

Now let's look at Mandhana Retail Ventures. The demerger finally happened on 14 December 2016. The very next day, the Big Bull bought 2.81 million shares of the company, which represented a 12.74 per cent stake in the company. The financials had been good thus far as revenue was up 22.4 per cent at Rs 117 crore for H1FY17, with margins at 25.2 per cent in H1FY17 versus 17.5 per cent in H1FY16.

On the retail side, the Being Human brand's first term of contract was to end in March 2020. The management was looking to renew it over the next six months for another term of nine years. Interestingly, royalty, which used to be at 3 per cent, rose to 5 per cent and was expected to go even higher in the future.

The brand closed FY16 with fifty-one exclusive stores in India and one in Nepal, with an eighty-store target by end of the calendar year. They were also said to be ready to tap new international markets. 'The aspirational value for Being Human is very high in tier II and tier III towns. These cities are growing and the disposable income is good because of which these become the focus area,' said Mandhana.[4] 'We would be adding celebrities from not just Bollywood but also from the sports world who are already the face of certain brands. We are exploring more celebrities in the lifestyle category for which we will buy the rights like we have done with the Salman Khan Foundation,' the company added.[5]

Everything seemed fine on the surface but cracks were starting to show. It was a secondary market transaction where the pledged shares of Mandhana Retail Ventures moved from lenders to Jhunjhunwala. This helped reduce promoters' loans.

Interestingly, according to the December 2016 BSE shareholding pattern report, it was seen that 73.6 lakh promoters' shares out of 94.14 lakh shares were pledged, meaning 78.2 per cent of promoter group shares were pledged in favour of lenders. The promoter and the promoter group held 42.6 per cent in the retail company as of the quarter ending December 2016. Manish Mandhana was said to be looking for other ways to reduce the residual loans. The management did clarify that no contingent liability would come to the retail company due to its parent; only Rs 17.5 crore was the retail portion of the loans which was given to Mandhana Retail Ventures. Rs 10 crore of this was paid, so Rs 7.12 crore was left. But still, the pledged shares concern was a big one because if the lenders didn't get paid back, they would openly sell the Mandhana Retail Ventures shares that they got as a part of the demerger in the open market, which would lead to huge depression in share prices. The parent company, Mandhana Industries, had debt of Rs 800 crore where bankers had invoked a Strategic Debt Restructuring (SDR), or the SDR from the RBI—which enabled banks who have issued loans to corporates to convert a part of the total outstanding loan amount and interest into major shareholding equity in the company.[6]

It was reported on 11 January 2018 that ChrysCapital, a leading India-focused private equity firm, picked up 3 per cent in Mandhana Retail through the secondary market. Shares were trading at Rs 200 at that point.

FY18 was again a good year for the company with 167 international stores, 610 points of sale, 57.3 per cent gross margin, 9,00,000 loyal customers and a plan to tie up with international retail giants in the US and South-east Asia to boost exports.

Sales had increased from Rs 172 crore to Rs 259 crore between FY15 and FY18. However, operating profit had reduced from Rs 44 crore to Rs 21 crore. PAT had reduced drastically from Rs 20 crore in FY17 to Rs 9.1 crore in FY18. Signs of the operational inefficiencies of the company were becoming visible. The royalties paid to Salman Khan had also recently doubled to 6 per cent from 3 per cent. It was worth noting that the director remuneration was quite high when compared to net profit in FY18.[7]

All hell broke loose on 5 April 2018. Salman Khan was found guilty in the 1998 black buck poaching case, after which the Mandhana Retail Ventures share lost 16 per cent in a single day.

Towards the end of 2018, after clocking an all-time high earlier, Mandhana Retail dropped to nearly Rs 100.

The company had plenty of problems to deal with.

In FY19, sales reduced to Rs 220 crore. There was a net loss of Rs 0.6 crore thanks to reduced sales and increasing finance costs. This further deteriorated in FY20. Sales reduced to Rs 152 crore with a loss of Rs 31 crore, again thanks to increased interest costs and depreciation.[8]

In FY20, a major disruption took place that no one had anticipated in their wildest dreams. The Being Human Foundation was transferring its business to another licensee. Mandhana Retail was forced to evaluate their options to start afresh but that again came with a catch. It had to be done post-pandemic as the whole world came to a standstill, with lockdowns everywhere. All the problems hit them at once. Mandhana Retail had no business operations post FY20. The sad part was that the annual report of FY20 stated that the licence agreement was perhaps drafted in a hurry and did not have the benefit of sound commercial and legal advice given how the terms of separation provided for transfer of designs, inventories and stores to the entity specified by the Being Human Trust (the licensor). The terms also provided for transfer of personnel.[9]

The story didn't end there. The auditors expressed concern regarding the company's going concern status given the termination of the Being Human licence agreement. In simple words, the auditors said that the company might not survive.

In FY21, sales reduced to a mere Rs 44 lakh. In FY21, there was a loss of Rs 3 crore. In FY22, sales increased to Rs 1 crore but losses mounted to Rs 5.4 crore. Despite the efforts of the management at exploring other options, nothing really took off.[10]

Big Bull's Story with Mandhana

The Big Bull faced massive losses in Mandhana Retail Ventures. While this was an off-market transaction, the acquisition price was expected to be near Rs 200.

Jhunjhunwala held 28.13 lakh shares, representing 12.74 per cent of the company, worth Rs 56 crore. The stock had listed on 14 December 2016 by hitting an upper circuit limit reaching Rs 227. Upper circuit implies the maximum price that a stock can trade at on a particular day.

Despite the Being Human brand termination, Rakesh maintained his stake till June 2021. The share price was Rs 5.10 on 23 March 2020. Then he started trimming. He trimmed it to 8.09 per cent on 26 September 2021. In October 2021 (from 5 or 7 October), through sale, he brought this down further to 2.40 per cent. And, finally, in the December 2021 quarter, Rakesh Jhunjhunwala's name was not visible in the shareholding pattern, which meant he had reduced his stake to less than 1 per cent or exited fully. Going by the rules, a listed company has to disclose the names of all the shareholders who hold more than 1 per cent stake in the company. The name of the company was further changed from Mandhana Retail Ventures Limited to Heads UP Ventures Limited with effect from 11 May 2022.

Today, the company's total market capitalization is Rs 30 crore, down from the peak of nearly Rs 500 crore. The market cap of the company is down by more than 90 per cent with Rakesh's loss estimated at more than Rs 50 crore (Rs 56 crore was the initial investment that was put in).

Part III

What You Can Learn from Rakesh Jhunjhunwala

Rakesh Jhunjhunwala, being the articulate fellow that he was, enjoyed interacting with students and stock market investors, sharing his pearls of wisdom. In one such interesting lecture at the FLAME University in Pune, he explained why the stock market exists. Despite having a history of over a hundred years, the stock market is still seen as a gambling den. The maturity and logic with which Rakesh explains the purpose of the stock market should be known to everyone who aspires to enter Dalal Street.

'Just after or during the industrial revolution, there arose the need for a large amount of capital. A single family couldn't have had it. Thus was born the idea of a joint stock company. People who owned shares in the joint stock company were diverse. They wanted a constant ability to sell these shares and have valuations for those.

Therefore arose the idea of a stock market and liquidity,' Rakesh said in the lecture at FLAME University.

'Stock market transfers capital from owners of the capital to those who can use the capital in order to provide liquidity and a mechanism by which this can be valued. The stock market exists to enter and exit from shares. It hasn't come because some people wanted to create a gambling den, as many people think. The stock market or capital market has a very big purpose. They are temples of capital allocation,' he added.

Rakesh was a true votary of capitalism. He felt that communism failed only because in it, the state had the monopoly on allocating capital, which led to its inefficient use. Market dynamics are much more powerful and efficient in allocating capital.

'Dhirubhai Ambani and Ratan Tata could not have become what they are had it not been for the public money and the stock market,' emphasizes Rakesh.

Now that the purpose of the stock market is clear, it's only natural to learn the lessons of stock market investment from the man himself.

Chapter 12

Inherent Optimism about India

Rakesh truly believed in the potential of India since the day he set foot in the stock market. He had all the money in the world to go global, that is, to look for investment opportunities beyond India. But forever an India bull, he believed more in the Indian story than any global story. In fact, he was averse to buying MNC stocks in his initial days. 'He would get miffed at us as to why we were buying MNC stocks. "*Tum log MNC stock kyon kharidta hai?* Indian companies *khatm ho gayi hai kya*? (Why do you people buy MNC stocks? Are there no Indian companies?)" he would tell us often,' recalls one of his old friends.

In an interview, he himself mentioned that Radhakishan Damani and he differed on many investment ideas, including MNCs. 'R.K. Damani would buy MNC stocks but I was averse to it. I don't want to be a husband of an unwilling wife. Let's face it. The fact is, MNCs don't want more shareholders,' Rakesh said in a 2015 lecture at

FLAME University. Later, he did invest in a few MNC stocks such as HUL, GlaxoSmithKline and Nestlé.

His inherent optimism about India is what earned him the title 'the Big Bull of India'. You just have to recall a difficult phase in the stock market and watch his interviews from those days. He had been a buyer in all of the bear phases that the stock market has seen, be it the dotcom bubble burst of 2000, the global financial crisis of 2008, the recent Covid-19 crash in March 2020 or the Russia–Ukraine war in 2022. 'In 2000, the dotcom bust had hurt Jhunjhunwala and Damani in a big way. Damani had had enough. He went on to launch the one-stop supermarket chain D-Mart while Jhunjhunwala invested back in the stock market whatever he was left with. Hardly any investor dared to take positions in the market during those days but he believed in India's growth story and potential in the stock market,' recalls his old friend.

His optimism paid him well. His wealth multiplied by many times during the bull market that had started after 2002. All the portfolio stocks that he had bought in the 1990s, especially Titan, turned multi-baggers during this phase. This is the phase that marked his shift from being a trader to a smart investor. 'In 2001–02, I realized India is on the threshold of a secular growth story and wrote so in the *Economic Times* in June 2001,' he said in the FLAME lecture.

When the 2009 crisis hit the stock markets, Rakesh kept his nerve. 'Now is the time to buy the riskiest assets. Risk is a word with many dimensions. But the way I see it—say I buy something for Rs 100. It could be that it becomes Rs 60 or Rs 70 or Rs 40. But the way I envisage things—can it be Rs 1200, can it be Rs 1300, can it be Rs 500 or Rs 400? What is the probability of the asset reaching those prices? I think the riskiest assets bought now can give you the greatest return provided you have the risk appetite, patience and it's your own, not borrowed, capital,' he told Sanjay Pugalia in an interview on CNBC Awaaz. Rakesh's bullishness on India rested on India's young population (favourable demographics) compared to other markets like the US, Europe and Japan and on India's low per capita income, which provided much scope for catching up to advanced economies. It was a difficult time to be bullish in 2002. The bull market didn't really gather steam till 2004. An investor looking back even in January 2005 would have seen a decade of just 5 per cent returns on the Sensex. 'The past decade has not been good,' Rakesh noted in an interview with NDTV in January 2005. 'Over the next five–ten years, the best investable asset would be equity. The thing that can disrupt this is the world economy such as the US or a hard landing in China,' he told the interviewer.

'The growth we've had in the NIFTY in the last ten years will be far exceeded in the next ten years. Most of us are attuned to the thought that this country cannot improve. We cannot grow at 10 per cent. We can't have a responsive administration. I think that will change. When I was doing my CA, we had a 95 per cent rate of income tax. Nobody thought income tax rates would go below 75 per cent. Now we have a 30 per cent rate of income tax,' he told Shereen Bhan of CNBC-TV18 in 2014 after the Modi election victory. 'India will see growth greater than China. We all will be surprised by the kind of growth that will come,

Mr Modi will be the instrument of change but the change will be incremental,' he added. According to Shankar Sharma, an investment guru and broker, some of Rakesh Jhunjhunwala's enthusiasm was simply a result of not having seen the world. Rakesh rarely travelled outside India or even outside the city of Mumbai. This insularity, somewhat counterintuitively, actually burnished his confidence in the country, according to Sharma.

Rakesh's optimism about India's growth was paired with his optimism about the returns on Indian stocks in the long run. There were moments of doubt, but these were quickly reversed. When the Covid-19 pandemic hit India, Rakesh became bearish for a while. 'I sold 2 per cent of my portfolio in March 2020 but in April–May, I changed my view and I took on the highest leverage of my life. The biggest bull market lies ahead of us,' he told Shekhar Gupta of ThePrint in a 2021 interview. Rakesh's optimism also transcended his political sympathies. 'I'm a patriotic Indian but I don't mix business with patriotism or business with pleasure,' he added in the same conversation with Shekhar. In various public pronouncements, Rakesh spoke approvingly of the Modi government. 'Mr Modi should lead this country for the next ten years,' he told Shereen Bhan in an interview with CNBC-TV18 in 2014. However, he continued to maintain that his confidence was not related to any particular government being in power. While speaking to the authors of this book, Shankar Sharma reiterated that this was Rakesh's best quality. 'Rakesh was extremely bullish on India but not bullish on any particular political dispensation taking India somewhere. In the last few years, it's all become mixed up, politics and investing, which I think is absolutely dangerous. Every pursuit is a completely independent pursuit, and you don't get involved in analysing a country necessarily through its politics. I say this goes for Harshad Mehta and Rakesh. They remained bullish on the whole India story itself. In Harshad's time we had Congress, then we had the United Front and then we had the NDA. I find that is a big lesson to all investors that don't get mixed up with your political inclination,' he said.

Similarly, he was not bullish on all sectors and stocks. He knew what would perform and what would not. While he believed in the broader growth story of India, he stayed away from a few spaces that he felt would not be rewarding. Rakesh did not extend his forever bullish view to tech stocks such as e-commerce, one of the most loved segments among retail investors in bull phases such as the late 1990s, 2014–15 or 2021–22. Speaking at the Economic Forum for India at the London School of Economics in 2015, Rakesh argued against this segment. 'We don't have to participate in every party. Pets.com burnt 500 million dollars in the last phase of the internet boom. I think e-commerce will grow more than what you expect but I don't want to buy these companies. Forget the valuation, where is the complete business model? I want to know Flipkart's business model. You want to lose 250 million dollars a year, where are you going? Where are the cash flows going to come (from)?' he asked. He was also cautious on 'flavour of the day' stocks such as private-sector banks in 2015.

His optimism rested on India being a democratic country that is open to accepting change and is tolerant. 'Democracy slows us down but it keeps it together. Look at the list of large-sized developed countries, which have prospered over the last fifty years or so. They have one quality in common, that is, they are all democratic. Anything can happen in a dictatorship . . . Indian democracy is maturing,' he said at a FLAME lecture in 2009.

He believed in Indians' skill of making the most of opportunities. 'In 1966–67, the government passed an order that GlaxoSmithKline (now GSK) and other multinational companies have to manufacture APIs in India. So they set up plants in India. That was the end of it. Now India is a leading manufacturer of APIs in the world. Now we are making it cheaper than foreigners. We have made atomic bombs indigenously. We haven't stolen technology from anyone. We have launched space satellites for Israel. We do it at 5 per cent cost at which NASA does it. We are a tolerant and skilled society with entrepreneurship in our culture,' Rakesh said in the same 2009 FLAME lecture.

Demographics are also playing in our favour. 'Every society goes through demographic evolution. For the next forty years, India is going to be among the most favourable demographic profiles of any substantial nation in the world. This cannot be reversed. All societies that have had the greatest prosperity have gone through this cycle. China is going to lose it fast due to their one-child policy,' he added. Rakesh observed these trends in 2009, and these views are relevant even today.

Fast forward to today. Rakesh's investment in India's newest airline, Akasa Air, is another testimony to his belief in India's growth story. Renowned billionaire entrepreneur Richard Branson has famously said, 'If you want to be a millionaire, start with a billion dollars and launch a new airline.' Many tycoons, from Vijay Mallya in India to Tony Fernandes in Malaysia, have lost their fortunes in airline businesses. Airline companies are hardly profitable. Even Warren Buffett sold all his airline stocks— United Airlines, American Airlines, Southwest Airlines and Delta Airlines—as all were in losses in 2020. Rakesh Jhunjhunwala, however, took a contrarian call by investing $200 million for 46 per cent stake in Akasa Air. 'Many people ask me why I have invested in an airline. I tell them that I am prepared for Akasa Air to even fail, but better to have tried and failed than not tried at all,' he said at an industry event in February 2022. 'I hope to prove people wrong. Now it's become a matter of ego,' he added.

Rakesh was last seen publicly at the launch of Akasa Air before he breathed his last. He confidently announced in interviews that being a frugal airline, Akasa Air would be very competitive in the aviation space.

'India's per capita discretionary expenditure will keep growing, so will the demand for flights. Therefore, there will be a lot more flights. Ministry for Civil Aviation has predicted that in four years, we'll go from 14 crore to 40 crore passengers flying a year. What does it mean? We need two-and-a-half times more aircraft every year. India's aircraft fleet size requirement will almost double by 2027 and it will need 1200 aircraft,' Rakesh said in an interview with CNBC-TV18 in August 2022.

What Rakesh believed is for all to see. The world is staring at a recession in which developed economies such as the US and Europe might log negative growth, but India is expected to grow at 6–7 per cent in FY23 and FY24, going by estimates from different agencies. In October 2022, international investment banker Morgan Stanley came out with a report saying the next decade belongs to India. It says that the four global trends of demographics, digitalization, decarbonization and deglobalization are favouring the New India, which is estimated to drive a fifth of global growth through the end of this decade. 'India has the conditions in place for an economic boom fuelled by offshoring, investment in manufacturing, the energy transition and the country's advanced digital infrastructure. These drivers will make it the world's third-largest economy and stock market before the end of the decade, we estimate,' says Morgan Stanley in its report titled 'The New India: Why This is India's Decade'.

Not very long ago, in 2021, Rakesh said, let alone the decade, the next *century* belongs to India.

'India has got some inherent qualities required for growth. We as a society have to tap those qualities and enable our citizens for growth. In the last three to four years, the reforms that have taken place in the form of Jan Dhan and the way Indian society has digitalized, ease of doing business and privatizing public sector companies are all going to lead to double-digit growth in India. India evolves and whatever evolves is permanent. India's growth is not top-down but it's all bottoms-up. I have the same views about India today as I had ten years ago and what I will have till the day I live . . . I don't know if most Indians are recognizing our country's potential, but at least Indian markets are recognizing it,' he said, addressing a gathering at the India Economic Conclave 2021.

In the same interview, the anchor, Nikunj Dalmia, asked Rakesh: 'If the ongoing bull market is on a train journey from Churchgate to Borivali, then where has the bull market reached?' 'It has reached Charni Road, which is the very next station after Churchgate,' Rakesh responded in a jiffy. What he implied was it was just the beginning of the bull market. Even in 2021, he knew the bull market would continue. Despite short-term hiccups due to the Russia–Ukraine war, the rout in global tech stocks and rate hikes by the US Federal Reserve and other central banks, the Indian markets hit a fresh high in November 2022.

Chapter 13

Patience and a Long-Term Outlook

The stock market is a place to make quick bucks. Right or wrong, this is a common perception. No wonder most people come here with a mindset to get rich quickly. They enter the market to trade, not to invest. Here lies the catch. Rakesh Jhunjhunwala didn't earn his fortunes through trading alone. It did play an integral role in him collecting money in the initial days, but the real wealth he accrued by investing the trading profits in quality stocks for the long term. Learning the tricks of the 'trade' is not an easy job, but investing is. The first and foremost principle of investing is having patience and a long-term outlook. One cannot be a great investor if one always thinks about buying and selling different stocks.

Jhunjhunwala was a visionary man since the early days, says a family friend who has known him since the late 1980s. 'He did tell many of us to take positions in Titan and CRISIL, but only he had the vision to hold it for years.

He could see its long-term potential and stood by it,' he said. Rakesh began investing in Titan Industries in the late 1980s, far earlier than the popular narrative of him buying the stock in 2002. Time and compounding powered returns not just in Titan but also in the overall portfolio. Rakesh set foot in the stock market in 1986. He is fabled to have begun with Rs 5000 in his pocket. His portfolio attained a value of approximately Rs 35,000 crore in 2022, at the time of his death. Some estimates put this value a lot higher. Debashis Basu put the worth of Rakesh's portfolio at Rs 50,000 crore in an article in *Moneylife*.[1]

* * *

According to Basu, with these two numbers, the compounded annual growth rate or CAGR for Rakesh works out to be either 62 per cent or 65 per cent—eye-popping numbers by any yardstick. In the long run, the return for the stock market as a whole is typically assumed to be just 12 per cent. As per Basu, Rakesh's returns make him the most successful investor in the history of investing, bar one—Jim Simmons of Renaissance Technologies, who notched up 66 per cent CAGR between 1988 and 2018, and ahead of the likes of George Soros, Stanley Druckenmiller and Warren Buffett. Ramesh Damani feels that this sort of record simply cannot be replicated. 'I've known Rakesh from 1988 to August 14, 2022. He compounded his wealth at 54 per cent over this period. In dollar terms, it is 47 per cent or something. So my feeling is that there's some records that stand the test of time. For example, Don Bradman's batting average,' Damani said.

To compare his portfolio's performance with the Sensex, in 1986, the benchmark Sensex was at 561 points. At the time of Rakesh Jhunjhunwala's death, it was 59,842. This is a growth of 106 times. If we were to work out the return rate for the Sensex, it would be 13.8 per cent CAGR. This nowhere matches Rakesh's CAGR, going from Rs 5000 to Rs 35,000 crore. Returns alone did not build Rakesh's fortune. He took on highly risky leveraged bets (borrowing) early in his career and this allowed his personal return to vastly exceed that of the Sensex. However, this was not all smooth sailing. In an interview with Ramesh Damani in 2011, Rakesh said that his trading profits came in fits and starts—getting supercharged in bull markets such as 2002–07 and 2014 onwards. However, there were periods, such as 1993 to 1999, when he did not make much money from trading. He had an almost superhuman patience with such periods. In an interview with Shekhar Gupta at ThePrint in 2021, he gave the example of his patience with shares in Hindustan Unilever (HUL). 'In 2001, at the index of 2900, HUL was at 327. Hindustan Unilever did not exceed that price for eleven years. Index went from 2900 to 22,000. Lever exceeded that price only in 2012. For eleven years, you had no returns except dividends. That's because in the preceding period, Lever had already run up,' he said.

Patience is another virtue that one must learn from him. His patience was legendary, something he often emphasized in his public interactions, and this was focused on company fundamentals rather than stock prices. 'As long as your company is gathering earnings, PE can come in three months. Earnings cannot come in three months.

There was no growth in the corporate sector in the stock market between 1999 and 2003. Once the markets started moving up, you got the PEs in just six months. As long as earnings are coming, have patience. People want to sell the flowers and water the weeds. People want to sell their profitable investments and keep the loss makers. Every exit should be an independent decision,' he told students at a lecture at FLAME University.

An unwarranted crash in a stock never bothered him. His Delhi-based stockbroker friend shares an interesting incident. When Britain voted to exit the European Union (popularly known as Brexit) in June 2016, it sent shockwaves across global markets. 'Bhaiya expected otherwise. He didn't think Brexit would happen. The verdict came out early in the morning. He told me that before he went to sleep, he instructed Rekha to not wake him. He must have made losses, but he reacted calmly and acted on it later in the day when the Brexit carnage on D-Street settled.'

Giving an example of a pharma company, Giving an example of a pharma company, a former employee, who didn't wish to be named, shared an interesting story. 'The pharma company was going through political turmoil, an issue unrelated to financial matters. The stock crashed, reacting to the news. Bhaiya had heavy stakes in it. He called us to ask about its fundamentals. We told him that numbers were strong. There was absolutely no financial risk to the company. He knew the stock had fallen more than it deserved. In a split second, he called his dealer and added more positions. After three to four days, a clarification was issued in connection with the political trouble in the company and the stock zoomed. Bhaiya made a lot of money and held on to its positions for the long term,' the ex-employee said.

Rakesh may have earned his fortunes through direct stock investment, but he advised common investors to take the mutual fund route. In an interview at the Times Network India Economic Conclave 2021 held in March, Rakesh spoke about how investing through mutual funds is a mature option for those not into the stock market full-time. It was in the context of 'Robin Hood' investors making money in stocks such as Gamestop around February 2021. We had its Indian variants in different stocks, when a lot of people opened their demat accounts after the Covid-19 crash and the subsequent bull run in the stock market. 'Don't involve yourself in all this gambling where stocks go up by 40 and 50 per cent every day. The mature attitude is to invest safely, give your money to experienced people to invest through mutual funds to fund managers and expect a reasonable return,' he said.[2]

The 'Mutual Funds *Sahi Hai*' campaign by AMFI has borne fruit, leading to a large number of investors now investing in mutual funds. But there is still a lack of personal experience in ordinary families in India about building wealth through SIPs or mutual funds. This is because the mutual fund industry is a relatively recent phenomenon. Mutual funds did exist in 1986 but these were all in the public sector and far different from the efficient, well-regulated vehicles they are today. For retail investors in 1986, there were no index funds in India that would have enabled you to invest in the thirty companies of Sensex in one go through the mutual fund route. The mutual funds that existed in the 1990s were usually close-ended vehicles. Close-ended means that the mutual fund collects money at a certain point and matures at a different point and in the interim, you are locked in. However, you can sell your units in the open market. This is different from open-ended funds (which are the dominant structure at present), where you can purchase and redeem your units with the fund house on any day. The close-ended structure would have reduced your liquidity. They also had a host of high upfront charges and this prevented them from being an efficient vehicle of wealth creation. What if you had picked the right stocks? Several blue-chip companies have been listed and traded since the beginning (with some changing their names or getting merged). Among these, you can count names like Tata Motors, ITC, Tata Steel, Larsen & Toubro, Reliance Industries, Grasim, Siemens, Hindustan Unilever and Mahindra and Mahindra. It is difficult to trace each of their prices in 1986. Some of them have acted as compounding machines and this is evident from more recent data as well. Hindustan Unilever was Rs 166 on 1 January 1999. Today, it is Rs 2600 (as of 23 August 2022). Mahindra and Mahindra traded at Rs 20.75 on 1 January 1999. Today, it is at Rs 1272 per share (a CAGR of 23 per cent). On the flip side, some companies would have gone into losses and ultimately gone bankrupt. The best example of this is a company like Mahanagar Telephone Nigam Limited (MTNL). It has gone from a price of Rs 183.4 on 1 January 1999 to Rs 21.80 at present (as of 5 October 2022). Reliance Communications (RCom) is another example. This Anil Ambani Group company was listed in 2006 with much fanfare. As the group took missteps with over-leveraging (excessive use of debt) and suffered from the fallout of regulatory actions, the stock price kept going south. Reliance Communications' shares have declined from Rs 300 on 10 March 2006 to trade at just Rs 2.25 at present (on 5 October 2022).

In today's investing environment, an index fund tracking the NIFTY or Sensex takes care of this 'churn'. An index fund is a passive mutual fund that simply invests in the same companies that comprise an index. For example, the NIFTY50 index fund will only invest in the fifty companies on the NIFTY50 index. Such investment vehicles were simply not available when Rakesh started and his ability to thrive despite the lack of sophistication is a testament to his genius. However, in today's more investor-friendly stock market, you do not need to be a genius to build up a nest egg for a comfortable retirement or save enough money for a good life. A portfolio having index funds in different categories, such as large-cap, mid-cap and small-cap, and a couple of debt mutual funds such as target maturity funds or liquid funds can do the trick. But if someone really wants to understand how Rakesh Jhunjhunwala made his money through trading, let's understand his risk management skills.

Chapter 14

Risk Management in Trading

Rakesh built his capital through trading in the initial stages of his life in the stock market. He did not start out with family money, nor did he have any intention to manage a fund or corpus for a third party to earn capital. He had no option but to trade and take leverage (borrow money) in order to take large bets on stocks. Leverage capital amplifies your buying power in the stock market, and that helps you make big money. How does leverage work? Let's understand leverage and non-leverage trading. Suppose you have Rs 2,00,000 to invest in stock A, whose spot price and futures price are the same, at Rs 400. You can take the following two actions:

i) Buying stock A in the cash market at the spot price
ii) Buying futures of stock A in the derivatives market

In the first situation, you will be able to purchase 500 shares of stock A. Now if the stock price goes up from Rs 400 to Rs 450, you will end up earning profits to the tune of Rs 25,000, a jump of 12.5 per cent. If the price drops to Rs 350 from Rs 400, then the losses you incur will stand at Rs 25,000.

Coming to the second situation, in the derivatives market, the futures are sold in lot sizes. Assume stock A has a lot size of 1000 shares. The contract value of one lot size will be Rs 400 * 1000 = Rs 4,00,000.

But you only have Rs 2,00,000 available with you. The beauty of the futures market is leverage trade, which is also known as margin trade. Your broker may provide you leverage (margin money), in which you only have to keep some margin with the broker. Suppose it is 30 per cent of the leverage. Now you only have to pay 30 per cent of Rs 4,00,000, which is Rs 1,20,000, to buy one lot of stock A futures. If the price moves from Rs 400 to Rs 450, you will make Rs 50,000 profits. You may have taken a bet on Rs 4 lakh but essentially, you invested just Rs 1.20 lakh to earn Rs 50,000 in profits. Your return on equity thus is 41.66 per cent (50,000/1,20,000). This is much better than what you could have earned in the cash market. Leverage thus amplifies your returns faster.

Trading with borrowed capital, however, is extremely risky. What if your trading call goes wrong? You will have to make up for the losses on the entire capital of Rs 4 lakh.

Rakesh Jhunjhunwala had set a rule for himself. '*Sar salamat to pagadi hazaar*'—Rakesh would often quote this one-liner. It means, better to sacrifice a little pride to save your life. He would never get emotionally attached to his trading bets. If his trading call went wrong, he would accept the loss and settle the trade the same day. It means that whatever he owed to his debtor, he would pay off and close the matter the same day. This ability to take losses made him the astute trader that he was. He would pay off the lender even if he suffered mark-to-market losses. 'He would tell us, never let lenders sit on our heads. It will affect you emotionally and may cripple your judgement during market hours,' says one of Rakesh's ex-employees.

'Most people feel ashamed if a trading call goes wrong, but Bhaiya was cut from a different cloth. He never cared about being right or wrong. His goal was to make money,' the ex-employee says.

'Whatever I have learnt in the stock market, I owe it to him. One of the finest lessons that I have learnt is when to scale up and down in trading. Bhaiya has a calculator in his mind. Mentally, he would fix a threshold of the leverage. If it went past it, he would ruthlessly sell. For example, if he was playing with Rs 10,000 crore, and he lost Rs 200–300 crore, he wouldn't care about his outlook on the stock. He would first sell and think about the next move later. Even if it seemed that the market would go up tomorrow, he would still sell.'

With all the money that he had, Rakesh could easily hold on to his loss-making trading bets and wait for them to make good, but he preferred to book losses rather than wait to flip the situation. In contrast, most people take on more leverage when they are making losses. This is a cardinal mistake.

Rakesh had tasted early on how borrowed capital may ruin one's fortunes in the stock market. In the early 1990s, during the first-ever bull market after the 1991 reforms, Harshad Mehta emerged as the poster boy of the stock market. Rakesh and Radhakishan Damani were still among the rookie traders under the patronage of Manu Manek, a big bear (someone who profits from a fall in stock prices) who was nicknamed Cobra. The bear camp believed that the exorbitant rally in the stock market was unwarranted. They dared to start selling shares in which Harshad was most active, such as ACC, Apollo Tyres, Mazda Industries, Karnataka Ball Bearings and Scindia Steamships, among others. At the onset of 1992 and after a great Budget by then Finance Minister Dr Manmohan Singh (when he opened up the economy to foreign investors), the markets were on fire, as if there were no tomorrow. The Manu Manek-led bear camp started selling stocks that they felt Harshad Mehta had artificially inflated. This is called short-selling, that is, selling shares that you don't own, anticipating the prices of the share will fall in the future. Once that happens, they can buy at a lower price and make delivery at a later date. What if the share doesn't fall and the settlement day for delivery arrives? If the seller cannot deliver shares, they need to pay *undha badla* (consideration for roll-over) to the buyer to roll over the delivery to the next settlement day. This is a unique situation in which the seller has to pay the buyer.

As the prices of Harshad Mehta's counters kept rising, the bear camp continued paying undha badla through borrowed capital. Rakesh would tell his friends later, had the rally continued for another couple of days, the bear camp and he would have been out of the market. It was purely luck, not skills, that saved the day for the bear camp. The first week of April 1992 was a life-and-death scenario for Rakesh. Luckily, the same week, journalist Sucheta Dalal broke the news about missing banker receipts from the State Bank of India. The defaulter was none other than Harshad Mehta. His counters, which the bear camp had short-sold, fell like a house of cards. Finally, they made money. This was one of their biggest jackpots. However, it did teach Rakesh to eat only what he could digest. They did the same in Dhirubhai Ambani's Reliance Industries in 1997. This time, they were unsuccessful. Dhirubhai Ambani won the battle while the bear camp decided to cut their losses.

Such risky trades taught Rakesh to manage his leveraged bets. He made a rule to bear losses and settle the dues with his financiers before the new trading day began. He stayed away from excessive leverage and taking undue risks.

One of his friends has an interesting story to share about the discipline he followed in leveraged bets. 'Once, he asked me to buy shares of Tata Tea (after the 1992 scam). I had only Rs 12,000. He warned me not to go overboard on leveraging. However, I went overboard against RJ's advice. I did make a profit of Rs 20 lakh (on Rs 12,000) by excessive leverage, but when I told Rakesh about this, he furiously told me to stay away from such risks. His point was to make money within limited risks. "*Sattebaji na kar* (do not gamble)"—that's what he told me,' the friend shares the anecdote.

Rakesh's friend made money on his suggested bet, but Rakesh didn't appreciate the way he did it. He took more risk than what was warranted. Nothing negative happened to the friend in this case, but he advised him to follow the rules. He preferred following a discipline in trading—knowing how much leverage to hold and when to exit. That is how he managed risk in leveraged trading.

According to investment guru Shankar Sharma, while speaking to the authors of this book, it is trading that built Rakesh's skill and these skills are something that managers of third-party money never quite develop. 'The pursuit of trading itself makes you a very rounded investor. You need that knowledge. If you're only an investor or managing money, you don't get to understand that. Ram Jethmalani was the greatest lawyer that the world has seen and probably will ever see. And I asked him once, what made you what you are? He replied that it's not that he's more intelligent than others but that he worked his way up by arguing criminal cases from the lowest court. According to Jethmalani, a criminal case in a lower court is not about law, it is about facts. What time did the accused leave, what colour shirt was he wearing—the lawyer needs to focus on minute details and this helped Jethmalani even while arguing a high-profile constitutional matter.' According to Sharma, 'Think of trading as being exactly that. There is an immediate feedback loop—at 3.30 p.m., you have a mark to market, which means you're extremely, extremely focused on the entire jigsaw of the market; you cannot afford to ignore anything.'

Rakesh's trading strategy was diametrically different from the 'buy low sell high' adage applied to investing. Rakesh would buy stocks that were trending or seeing momentum behind them, even if that meant buying at higher prices. Conversely, he would get out of stocks that were trending lower, even if it meant taking a loss. He fleshed out this thinking in a conversation with Ramesh Damani, broadcast on CNBC-TV18 in 2010–11.

'See, Ramesh, we don't initiate more than 40 per cent of trades that turn out to be right. We do what I call pyramiding. I buy a stock at Rs 100, I buy more at 105, I buy more at 110. So what is trading? It is basically momentum. You play with momentum. If the market is rising, buy on the rise. If markets are going down, you sell in the fall. This applies to short-term, medium-term and long-term trends. If you average a losing trading position, it is at your own cost. At least, I never do that. Suppose a stock is at 90 and I feel it's going to have a big upside and the fall is 4–5 per cent, I might average. As a rule in trading, I will never average. A good trader should have his highest position outstanding at the highest price. Who knows what is the highest price?' he said. According to Rakesh, that's why out of one million, only ninety or a hundred make money.

The bull market of 1992 during the Harshad Mehta days was not the only occasion when Rakesh was on the brink of losing it all in his trading calls. Another such occasion came ten years later, in 2002, when he turned prematurely bullish on the stock market. According to Sharma, Rakesh was in a tough spot in that year. 'There was a setback in June 2002. I had to liquidate 25 per cent of my portfolio in four days. But I did that, I honoured everything. When the markets turned favourable again, I leveraged again,' he said in a conversation with Ramesh Damani on CNBC in 2020.

Success in trading is inextricably connected to limiting one's losses in losing trades because not all trades will work out, even for the best traders. 'Know how to take a loss. Nobody can predict momentum. All big moves start with small moves. The price is the first indicator of what is coming. If I buy a stock at Rs 100, if it goes to 120, I buy more. If it goes to 90, I'm all squared up. I can't sleep, I can't eat, I have unease. Not every year I make money. I make money in spurts, like 1989–92, 2003–07, 2009–11. In the years 1994 to 1999, I would not have made any trading companies,' Rakesh added in his conversation with Damani. The need to control losses is particularly important because trading is largely funding by debt (borrowing). This applied to Rakesh Jhunjhunwala as well. 'We are not employing millions of dollars in trading. My net capital employed in trading is Rs 1 lakh. Everything else is borrowed. I borrow money against my and my wife's assets,' he told Damani.

Rakesh drew a sharp distinction between trading and investing. 'How do you find value in a stock? For every buyer, there is a seller. Some like Nandita Sen, some like Sushmita Sen, some like Aishwarya Rai. When you think of buying a stock, think of the business model. I'm talking about investing here, not trading. Would I have invested in Titan if I had not felt that the branded jewellery market in India will go from 5 per cent to 20 per cent? In five years, if 1 lakh crore is going to be the jewellery market in India, the branded jewellery in India will go from 5000 crore to 20,000 crore,' he told students at a lecture at FLAME University. Rakesh went on to elaborate what he meant by opportunity. 'When you look at the opportunity, look at the addressable opportunity. In infrastructure, the opportunity is huge, but if my company can only make water pumps, that's not good enough. The unknowns—to make them known is difficult,' he said.

According to Rakesh, another major difference between trading and investing is the concept of 'averaging down'. When the price of a share that you have bought falls, should you buy more at a lower price?' Rakesh answered this question at a Moneybee event in 2016. 'When you are trading, never average. Trading is about momentum. When you are investing, you can average. I have done so at times,' he said. When a stock moves against you in a trade, it means that the momentum is against you. In such a situation, averaging out your price can only compound your losses. In this situation, accepting the loss and getting out of the trade may be a smarter strategy. 'Small investors and those who do not have a deep understanding of the market should stick to mutual funds. If you want to invest in both mutual funds and direct stocks, allocate 95 per cent of your portfolio to mutual funds and only 5 per cent to stocks. Invest through SIPs because it is difficult to time the market,' he added.

In trading, he advised catching the momentum. He would always say, 'Trading is *vadhare vadhare, levanu; ghatade ghatade, vechvanu* (buy more if it's going up; sell if it's going down).' One has to be emotionless in trading bets. If a trading bet moves against your expectation, you accept the loss and move on. Respect the momentum.

'Trading is all about price. You need to have a broad direction of the market. You need not be an expert about it. You should know when to stake money and when to take a loss. What happens is, people try to extract too precise a trend rather than broadly recognizing the trend,' Rakesh said in an interview with Ramesh Damani.

In the same interview, Damani asked him if, given a choice, he would want to be a trader or an investor. 'I would want to be both. Both have its own pleasures. Trading profits have greater pleasure though,' Rakesh replied.

As far as retail investors go, Rakesh's advice was nuanced. He felt that ordinary investors had unrealistic expectations from equity as an asset class and while looking at stocks, people had a trading mentality rather than an investing mentality. In an interview with ValueQuest before the 2014 elections, he was asked if ordinary investors should invest in equities. 'Yes. I'll give you a very good example. When you buy an insurance policy from an agent, what dream does he sell you? Every month you give Rs 5000 and after a certain number of years, you'll get a lump sum. 40 per cent of the first premium goes as commission and after that 4–5 per cent commission. Why don't people have the same attitude about equities? People don't have realistic expectations. People don't know that the world's greatest investor has compounded wealth at 22 per cent,' he said. 'Trade is for creating capital, investing is for growth. In trading, the risk is extreme. Most people think they are investing but, in their mind, they're thinking about trading. If the return in other asset classes is 10–11 per cent, equity can give you 18 per cent. If I get 18 per cent, I'm a king, if I get 22 per cent, I'm an emperor. You get much greater returns than insurance. In 2002, I used to catch people on the road—sell your wife's bangles and buy equities (meaning that equities are so attractive, sell your wife's bangles if you need to, to find money to invest)—but nobody used to buy. If you want to trade, don't mix it with investing,' he said.

Chapter 15

Rakesh Jhunjhunwala's Mantra to Pick Stocks

Be an original thinker

To the people who followed his portfolio, Rakesh was categorical. 'You cannot make money on borrowed knowledge. Please understand what I'm saying and my thought process instead. Let me give you an example. I bought Sterling Holiday Resorts at 75 rupees. The stock immediately went to Rs 120 and now it is languishing at Rs 80. Those poor people have lost money. I personally have a five-year or seven-year time horizon, you haven't. I have a risk appetite that is much larger than yours. Don't try and do what I'm doing,' he told the interviewer at ET Now on 2 October 2012.

Consistency is key in the investment world and it comes only with one's conviction. 'Rakesh would never shy away from sharing his stock ideas with others. This is even when most of us, including R.K. Damani and Nemish Shah, would tell him not to. He would offer stock tips to even those who would come to him at Geoffrey's, where he would often go to hang out after market hours,' says Rakesh's trader friend.

Rakesh Jhunjhunwala called himself an open book. He couldn't have changed his character. He anyway knew that just knowing the stock idea was not enough. When to exit is equally important. The person who has suggested the stock idea will most likely make the smart exit, but he won't come back to tell you to do the same. This is the reason why investing on borrowed knowledge doesn't work. Sometimes Rakesh's views wouldn't gel with his friends R.K. Damani's or Nemish Shah's, but he would stick to his thought process. He would never get influenced.

Every Jhunjhunwala follower wants to learn how he picks his stock bets. This is what he has to say about it: 'Stock market investment cannot be taught. It has to be learnt.' It's not that he has never discussed his stock-picking mantra. It's about how well you receive the crux of it—more importantly, how you are going to practise it. There are five aspects which, according to Jhunjhunwala, should be followed to pick multi-bagger stocks:

i) Keep an open mind

Be receptive to what the world is showing you. By 'keep an open mind', Rakesh means that one has to observe their surroundings. Some of the great stock ideas come when you least expect it. Your observation about how everyone is using a certain technology, product or service and which listed player is behind it can help you land great stock opportunities.

ii) Opportunity

Second, one needs to assess the market opportunity as to how big an opportunity the company is looking at as its market size grows. The opportunity and market size should move in tandem. This is what provides a long runway for growth. There has to be a big change or a turnaround happening. The greatest wealth is earned when change happens, Rakesh would say. The business model should have entry barriers.

iii) Corporate governance

Corporate governance is about the management and how someone runs their company—their behaviour with their staff, vendors, distributors and others and their behaviour with money. Are they running their business with frugality? One needs to look into this stuff. A hard-working and honest management is important. Rakesh excelled at studying people and betting on them. Why he loved Tata Group stocks was only because of the sheer integrity of the management.

iv) Competitive ability

The company must have something superior in terms of competition against its peers, be it the brand, technology or capital. It should be a market leader.

v) Valuations

Finally, there is the price at which you are buying it. Even a great company bought at the wrong price (high valuations) will hurt your returns. So, price is important. Learn to value a company. Read valuations.

vi) Constant monitoring

Even though a long-term investor, he would keep monitoring how his portfolio companies were performing. He would often turn up in investor calls to quiz the management about the business prospects or other actions. If he felt the initial thesis was failing or the business model hadn't turned out the way he anticipated, he would prefer to sell his stakes.

When exactly should one sell an investment? Let's hear from Rakesh himself: 'As far as selling goes, I sell if a better opportunity comes along that will give me more value for money from what I am getting now. I will sell when I feel the stock has peaked or the business opportunity has peaked out. Selling should be an independent decision. It shouldn't be linked to how the stock market is doing. Don't flower your weeds and cut your roses. *Maine kasam khayi ki nuksaan mein nahi bechunga ki* is bullshit (I have sworn that I won't take a loss and sell—this is bullshit),' Rakesh points out in one of the TV interviews.

Chapter 16

What Not to Learn from Rakesh Jhunjhunwala

Rakesh Jhunjhunwala enjoyed a cult following in the stock market. Whatever he bought, sold or said on TV channels became headlines. People wanted to listen to him to learn from him. We have already compiled a list of things that you can learn from him. However, one cannot copy him completely. Some of the traits he possessed were unique to him and cannot be emulated. His leverage-driven investment style was too risky. It is just that he managed to handle his risks well. Not everyone can be as astute and as disciplined as he was in his investment process. We shall now discuss the things you should not learn from Rakesh:

Leveraged trading

Rakesh would borrow money to invest in the market so that he could take large positions for larger profits.

While he could manage his debt, he never advised others to follow this approach. Investing in the stock market on borrowed capital is one of the sure-shot ways to get poorer. In fact, in his keynote address to students at FLAME University in 2009, he talked about his wish to reduce his debt. 'I want to get deleveraged, but *hota nahi hai* (it's hard to do it). If I have bank balance, I can't sleep well. If I pay interest, then only I get good sleep,' he says.

It had become a habit for Rakesh to invest on borrowed capital and pay interest. In fact, in one of his interviews with Ramesh Damani, he claimed that he had deployed only Rs 1 lakh in trading; the rest was the borrowed capital. He boldly claimed often that he earned his wealth from the long-term investment through trading. Rakesh's story may inspire you to do the same. However, it is not meant for all. For him, it was a passion. This is what he did, thought and talked about all the time. He mastered it. A regular investor, whose primary job is different, will not have the time and the mindspace to emulate Rakesh's trading style.

For retail investors, borrowing to trade is not a great strategy. The market can be irrational in the short run, longer than you can stay solvent—even if you've made the right bets. Leverage forces you to either book a profit or get out of a trade in the short run. Without leverage, what would your returns have been? Let's understand with an example of the Sensex. A sum of Rs 561 invested in the Sensex from 1986 to 2022 would have become Rs 59,842 on 16 August 2022. But most people get regular monthly income from a salary and they tend to invest every month through an SIP rather than starting off with a lump sum amount and never adding to it. So if you had set up a simple SIP of

Rs 5000 per month in the Sensex over this period, it would have built a corpus of Rs 6 crore. If you had increased this SIP by 10 per cent every year, the money would have grown to 13.1 crore. Do these amounts seem low to you? You may know middle-class families who have built much more wealth than this by investing similar amounts twenty or thirty years ago in plots of land or flats. However, the secret to their fortune is also the same as Rakesh Jhunjhunwala's—leverage of debt. The typical home buyer would put down 20–30 per cent of the cost of the property as down payment and pay off the rest. This increases your starting capital. Let's assume that you bought a house for Rs 20 lakh in 1993 and put down Rs 5 lakh of your own money and borrowed the rest from a bank (Rs 15 lakh). The value of this house grows at a rate of 12 per cent over the next thirty years and your interest rate over the same period is 10 per cent. The value of this house would now be Rs 6 crore. Even adjusting for loan repayment with interest (a total payment of Rs 47 lakh if you had opted for thirty years), this value is much higher than a stock portfolio that grows at 12 per cent over the same period. A stock portfolio of Rs 5 lakh growing at 12 per cent over thirty years would attain a value of 1.5 crore. Why did this happen? The loan of Rs 15 lakh acted as a magnifier—it pushed up your overall wealth creation. However, leverage is by no means a good thing. A problem with the underlying asset—let's say a land dispute in the case of real estate or an undelivered flat—can send leverage into reverse, magnifying your losses rather than your profits.

Legendary investor Warren Buffett once said, 'When you combine ignorance and leverage, you get some pretty interesting results.' Leverage, if used well, magnifies your gains, but if used carelessly, it can magnify your losses dramatically. Losses not only affect your financial health but also devastate your mental wealth. One needs to be in sync with one's psychological behaviour to master trading. Even Rakesh would sometimes get frustrated if a trading bet worked against him. He was known to have thrown objects around, breaking glass tables and televisions if he incurred huge losses in trading. It's hard to maintain your calm seeing losses in your book. It makes you err more.

'Leverage is like a personal habit of smoking and drinking. If done in a measured manner, it's a pleasure. If overdone, it's a problem. It has to be emotionless. If it goes against you, nobody will come to help you,' says Rakesh in one of the TV interviews.

The timing of the leverage matters a lot as well. Not all can get it right. 'In 2002, even though I was extremely bullish on the stock market, I still sold 25 per cent of my portfolio in four days to reduce my leverage because one never knows what may happen. So get it right—there are times when you should leverage and when not . . . even though I had much more wealth in 2008 compared to what I had in 2003, the leverage in 2008 was not even 10 per cent of what I had in 2003. Timing and valuations matter,' Rakesh explained in an interview.

He often said that if things went against one's expectations, then it was better to square off and sit at home. The crux is to never let leverage control your trade. You control your leverage; the leverage should not control you. If one can master this art, one has arrived in trading the way Rakesh did.

Concentration—of asset class and stocks

Ask Rakesh Jhunjhunwala about his alternate career choice and 'There isn't any,' he would promptly respond. He proudly called himself a trader and investor. Rakesh was truly bullish about the Indian stock market and his own potential to make money through direct stock investment. He loved every bit of it. '98 per cent of my money is invested in equities,' he would often say in interviews.

This is in stark contrast to the basic principles of financial planning, which include allocating investments in different asset classes as per age, life goals and risk appetite, and rebalancing it periodically as and when the need arises. For example, if equities have had a strong bull run, their weightage in one's portfolio should have gone beyond what was decided upon earlier. It is a signal to sell equities and buy other asset classes to rebalance the portfolio to its original shape.

Rakesh, however, irrespective of the bear or bull phase in the stock market, stayed invested in equities completely. This is something a retail investor should never pursue. Rakesh may not have followed the principle of asset allocation himself, but he spoke highly of it in various interviews.

'First task of an investor is asset allocation. Why invest only in equities? There are other asset classes such as debt, equity, gold, land or art. Don't put all your money in equities just because Rakesh Jhunjhunwala does it. 60 per cent of your gains result from allocation of assets and 40 per cent from specific assets,' he said in his address to FLAME University students.

He preferred to stick to his knitting. Rakesh was often asked about other asset classes such as gold, real estate and fixed income in relation to stocks. His answer, given in several interviews, such as the one to ET Now on 2 October 2012, was the same. 'My wife knows about gold and invests in it. I do not. I don't have any fixed income—instead, I pay interest because I'm leveraged. As for real estate, I don't invest in it because it is very hard to manage. All kinds of government authorities are involved. I don't want to worry; tomorrow some inspector will come or some politician will come,' he said to the interviewer at ET Now. He very famously sold shares in CRISIL Ltd in 2005–06 worth about Rs 27 crore to buy a house. In February 2022, he told Anuj Puri, group chairman of Anarock, at a CII-organized real estate conference, that his house had appreciated to Rs 45 crore but if he had held on to the shares, they would be around Rs 1000 crore in value.

The same logic applies to his approach of having a concentrated portfolio, that is, allocating a high percentage of money to a smaller set of stocks in which one has high conviction. This is again a high-risk high-reward strategy meant for astute investors. A large part of his wealth was allocated to just three or four stocks such as Titan, Lupin and CRISIL. The rest of the stocks made for a small percentage. Having such a concentrated portfolio, where three or four stocks rule the roost, may not work for a regular investor. A diversified portfolio spread across different sectors and market capitalization makes for an ideal portfolio. Jhunjhunwala was able to make money through his concentrated bets, but not all can do it.

'I have questioned myself in the last two–three years as to why 100 per cent of my wealth should be in equities; why not debt, real estate or a business? I came to a conclusion that if India's nominal gross domestic product has to grow at 12 per cent, I will keep getting tax-free returns. I don't think any other asset class can give me such kind of returns. Second, my investments such as Lupin or Titan, I don't think their potentialities have been achieved. I will not sell them,' Rakesh said in a 2015 interview.

Small-cap bias

Rakesh Jhunjhunwala excelled at picking companies at the initial stage of their growth cycle. That said, he had a small-cap bias in his approach to picking stocks. More than 5000 companies are listed in the stock market. The large-cap stocks, comprising the top 100 in terms of market capitalization, are known to all and are well-researched. The next 150 stocks, between 101 and 250, are mid-cap stocks. Stocks having a ranking of 251 and beyond in terms of market capitalization comprise the small-cap universe. This is the segment where the magic happens. Rakesh was smart enough to pick quality stocks from the small-cap basket. He latched on to Titan, CRISIL and Lupin when these stocks were small-cap companies. 'It doesn't take me much time to make an investment decision. I can do it in ten minutes. I don't buy all positions in one go. I buy some, wait to see how the company performs, research more and then I increase my holdings,' says Rakesh.

A regular investor would do well to stay away from the small-cap universe as a beginner. The volatility in small-cap stocks may not let most investors sleep. Rakesh had a long-term vision and conviction in his stock picks. Even if a stock fell by 50 per cent, he would hold on to it if he was convinced that the fundamentals hadn't changed. Doing that may not be easy for a regular investor. If one wants to find multi-baggers from the small-cap universe, one has to spot it themselves. Only then can one have the discipline and belief to hold it for the long term and bask in its profitable glory.

One may feel that Rakesh had undue access to information that made him take informed calls when it came to stock picks. Rakesh categorically denies it. According to him, there is no information asymmetry in the market. 'Tamil Nadu state government offered to sell 25 per cent stake in Titan but Tatas didn't buy it. The truth is some of my finest investments are in companies where even management didn't have the confidence or vision that they will grow so much.' Titan is a joint venture between Tata Group and the Tamil Nadu Industrial Development Corporation Ltd.

Rakesh has said in different interviews that promoters of small-cap companies would come to him and tell him to 'manage' the price. 'They will say, the stock is at Rs 70, we shall give it to you at Rs 40. If you buy it, more people will follow you. This is how we'll take the prices upwards. Then you sell it. The kind of money such a scheme can make is humongous, but means are important. I would tell them I know the way to Arthur (Road) Jail. Don't tell me how to reach there,' he said.

Murky deals, price manipulation and forged financial results are all too common in the small-cap universe. Most of these companies do not even conduct earnings calls after the quarterly results. One has to invest in such companies with a pinch of salt. Finding gems in this space is not an easy task. It is better to leave it to the fund manager. Investing in a small-cap mutual fund would be much safer than picking small-cap stocks on one's own.

Taking health lightly

Rakesh Jhunjhunwala never liked to be compared with Warren Buffett, but comparisons are bound to happen for context. One major difference between Jhunjhunwala and Buffett was personal discipline towards health. Warren Buffett maintains his health. It is commonly known that Buffett earned 99.7 per cent of his wealth after his fifty-second birthday. He is ninety-two years old. Why is that so? It is the magic of compounding, where you keep earning returns on returns, which inflates your wealth at a faster pace as years go by. Rakesh Jhunjhunwala was successful by any measure. In his own words, he had far more wealth than he needed. However, if he had lived longer, the compounding effect on his wealth would have been eye-shattering. So, if you want to be a great investor, work on your health. Aim to live longer to let compounding work for you.

'If I were to make money in life again, would I want it to be any different? I don't think so. I enjoy standing on Dalal Street and fighting for wealth and success. I love trading. If God comes to take my life, I'll tell him to hold on for a day. Let me wake up at 7 a.m., do my yoga, have a cigarette and breakfast and tea. Then "*le phataphat de phataphat* (buy quickly, sell quickly)" when the market opens. Then Utpal would say, this company has had a dynamic change. I'll invest in that company and then I'll take three or four pegs at Geoffrey's and a good meal at home. Then I'll tell the Almighty to take me away,' said Rakesh at a lecture in 2015.

The man wasn't scared of death. He lived his life to the fullest, at his best. '*Mera bhagvan chala gaya* (my god is no more),' Rakesh would say after the demise of Nirmal Bang, the founder of Nirmal Bang Group, who died young, in the 1990s. Many from the stock market feel the same way about Rakesh. *Dalal Street ka bhagvan chala gaya*! May he rest in peace. May his wisdom and learnings live on.

Appendix

Rakesh Jhunjhunwala's Portfolio
(December 2022)

Company	(Figures in Rs crore)
Titan Company Ltd	12,487.70
Star Health and Allied Insurance Company Ltd	5,901.70
Metro Brands Ltd	3,378.80
Tata Motors Ltd	1,403.90
Canara Bank	1,204.80
CRISIL Ltd	1,176.50
Fortis Healthcare Ltd	1,001.30
Indian Hotels Company Ltd	931.4
NCC Ltd	746.9
Federal Bank Ltd	736.5
Aptech Ltd	689.1

Company	(Figures in Rs crore)
Tata Communications Ltd	607
Rallis India Ltd	433.3
Escorts Kubota Ltd	396.3
Jubilant Pharmova Ltd	387.4
Karur Vysya Bank Ltd	385
Nazara Technologies Ltd	379.4
Jubilant Ingrevia Ltd	266.6
Va Tech Wabag Ltd.	165.5
Agro Tech Foods Ltd	164.7
Anant Raj Ltd	116.5
Edelweiss Financial Services Ltd	89.4
Geojit Financial Services Ltd	85
Wockhardt Ltd	68.7
Dishman Carbogen Amcis Ltd	46
DB Realty Ltd	44.3
Singer India Ltd	35.1
Orient Cement Ltd	34.4
Man Infraconstruction Ltd	32.8
Prozone Intu Properties Ltd	9.8
Total	**Rs 33,406 crore**

This is based on mandatory disclosures of shareholders by companies who hold more than 1 per cent in that company compiled by Trendlyne. There could be some Jhunjhunwala holdings that are below 1 per cent in various companies—but this cannot be assembled from public sources. This does not include any unlisted companies, such as Akasa Air and any holdings in the name of Rekha Jhunjhunwala.

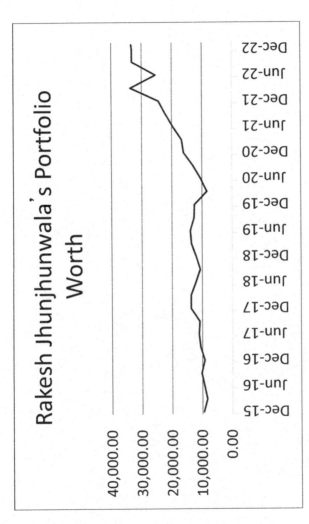

Rakesh Jhunjhunwala's Portfolio Worth

Source: Trendlyne

Excluding holdings in the name of Rekha Jhunjhunwala.

Acknowledgements

We started writing this book after the legendary Rakesh Jhunjhunwala passed away on 14 August 2022. In this time of grief, a lot of market experts, friends, former employees and associates of Rakesh took out the time to meet us and speak to us. In particular, we would like to thank ace investors Ramesh Damani, Shankar Sharma and Samir Arora who took out time from their busy schedules. We would like to thank Satya Sontanam, senior content creator, Livemint, for reading our book in record time and giving us a ton of helpful tips. We also acknowledge the work of the many journalists and anchors who interviewed Rakesh over the years, providing us with a rich storehouse of material to understand the Big Bull of Dalal Street.

Notes

Chapter 1: The Early Years

1 Mohammed Shahnawaz, 'Wizards of Dalal Street Disc1 Seq2 Part 2.' *YouTube* video, 0:43. 8 March 2011. https://www.youtube.com/watch?v=yRw89gqhkgg

Chapter 3: Trader versus Investor

1 Anil Manchanda, 'Rakesh Jhunjhunwala and Titan: His First Big Call', *The Hindu Businessline*, 15 August 2022, https://www.thehindubusinessline.com/companies/rakesh-jhunjhunwala-and-titan-his-first-big-call/article65769002.ece

Chapter 4: Being Legit in the Stock Market: The Years after the Tech Bust

1 CBNC Awaaz, 'Market Outlook 2009: Rakesh Jhunjhunwala 1.' *YouTube* video, 6:51. 26 December 2008, https://www.youtube.com/watch?v=nBhckYarLNA

2 'The Election of This Government Is Nothing but the Maturity of Indian Democracy: Rakesh Jhunjhunwala,' *The Economic Times*, 24 June 2014, https://economictimes.indiatimes.com/opinion/interviews/the-election-of-this-government-is-nothing-but-the-maturity-of-indian-democracy-rakesh-jhunjhunwala/articleshow/37115492.cms?from=mdr

3 Ashish Agashe, 'Jhunjhunwala: The RARE Big Bull and Unabashed Wealth Creator', rediff.com, 14 August 2022, https://www.rediff.com/business/report/jhunjhunwala-the-rare-big-bull-and-unabashed-wealth-creator/20220814.htm

Chapter 5: Investment Musings

1 Fenil Seta, 'EXCLUSIVE: "Rakesh Jhunjhunwala had the vision to back a film like English Vinglish at that point in time when many in the industry didn't have the confidence to do so" —R. Balki.' Bollywood Hungama, 14 August 2022. https://www.bollywoodhungama.com/news/features/exclusive-rakesh-jhunjhunwala-vision-back-film-like-english-vinglish-point-time-many-industry-didnt-confidence/

Chapter 6: The Story of Titan

1 Vinay Kamath, *Titan: The Story of India's Most Successful Consumer Company*, 20 December 2018.

2 Ravi Dharamshi, 'Rakesh Jhunjhunwala Interview with ValueQuest – After Rupee Crisis and before 2014 Elections.' *YouTube* video, 1:01:15. 19 August 2022. https://www.youtube.com/watch?v=QaWanFCu76M

3 Ibid.

4 Asit Manohar, '₹3 to ₹2535: Tata Stock Turns ₹1 lakh to ₹169 Crore in 20 Years', Mint, 29 August 2022, https://www.livemint.com/market/stock-market-news/rs-3-to-rs-2535-titan-company-shares-turn-rs-1-lakh-to-rs-169-crore-in-20-years-11661745382863.html

5 Titan Industries Limited, Annual Report, 1996–97, https://www.titancompany.in/sites/default/files/Annual%20Report%201996%20-%201997.pdf

Chapter 7: CRISIL

1 Mudar Patherya, 'Remembering Rakesh Jhunjhunwala: There Was No Moderation in His Existence,' *The Economic Times*, 14 August 2022, https://economictimes.indiatimes.com/markets/stocks/news/remembering-rj-there-was-no-moderation-in-his-existence/articleshow/93557908.cms?utm_source=contentofinterest&utm_medium=text&utm_campaign=cppst

2 Hemanth Gorur and Sumit Chowdhury, *Doing What Is Right: The CRISIL Story*, 10 December 2012.

3 Rajesh Mascarenhas, '5 Stocks and the Making of the Legend of Big Bull,' *The Economic Times*, 15 August 2022, https://economictimes.indiatimes.com/markets/stocks/news/five-stocks-and-the-making-of-the-legend-of-big-bull/articleshow/93566657.cms?utm_source=contentofinterest&utm_medium=text&utm_campaign=cppst

Chapter 8: Lupin

1 Disruption Series, Vol. 12, Pharmaceutical Industry, Ambit Capital, April 2021, p.2, https://www.ambit.

co/public/thought_leadership/Ambit_Disruption_
VOL12_Pharma.pdf

2 'Our Story', from the Lupin website, https://www.lupin.
   com/about-us/our-story/

3 Lupin   annual   report—https://www.bseindia.com/
   bseplus/AnnualReport/500257/73654500257.pdf

4 Shalini Rath, 'Lupin Limited | Success Story of Becoming
   a Multinational Pharma Company', startuptalky.com, 19
   October 2022, https://startuptalky.com/lupin-success-
   story/

5 S.P. Jain Institute of Management and Research, 'Dr.
   Kamal Sharma of Lupin Limited is Executive-in-
   Residence at SPJIMR', prnewswire.com, 2 December
   2016,   https://www.prnewswire.com/in/news-releases/
   dr-kamal-sharma-of-lupin-limited-is-executive-in-
   residence-at-spjimr-604219466.html

6 Suprotip Ghosh, 'K.K. Sharma's Skills Have Steered
   Lupin into Big Pharma League', *Business Today*, 5
   January 2014, https://www.businesstoday.in/magazine/
   cover-story/story/india-best-ceo-2013-pharma-kk-
   sharma-lupin-success-42614-2013-12-23

7 Disruption Series, Vol. 12, Pharmaceutical Industry,
   Ambit Capital, April 2021, p.2, https://www.ambit.
   co/public/thought_leadership/Ambit_Disruption_
   VOL12_Pharma.pdf

8 Ibid.

9 Sohini Das, Lupin's Goa Plant Gets 7 Observations
   from   Usfda,   Firm   Unperturbed,'   Business
   Standard,   19   September   2021,   https://www.

business-standard.com/article/companies/lupin-s-goa-plant-gets-7-observations-from-usfda-firm-unperturbed-121091900777_1.html; Monal Sanghvi, 'U.S. FDA Flags Quality Lapses at Lupin's Goa Facility', BQ Prime, 27 September 2021, https://www.bqprime.com/markets/us-fda-flags-quality-lapses-at-lupins-goa-facility (As per JM Financial brokerage, it is negative and broadly speaking, a plant getting repeat observations shows a lax approach to compliance.)

10 September 2017 Investor PPT of Lupin, Slide 5 titled 'Is the Indian Pharma Market Model done? - Current Model Showing Signs of Ageing', https://www.bseindia.com/xml-data/corpfiling/CorpAttachment/2017/9/a537fc59-a539-4b0e-899f-aa3fdb9785dd.pdf

11 Taken from a report titled 'India Pharmaceuticals—Favorable risk reward' by Vishal Manchanda and Bezad Deboo, published by Systematix on 20 September 2022.

12 Leroy Leo, 'Lupin Posts Rs 835 Crore Loss in Oct-Dec on Second Gavis Impairment,' Livemint, 6 February 2020, https://www.livemint.com/companies/company-results/lupin-posts-rs835-crore-loss-in-oct-dec-on-second-gavis-impairment-11581001557755.html

13 Harshita Singh, 'Stocks to Watch: ITC, Lupin, Ruchi Soya, Manappuram Finance, JSW, Biocon', *Business Standard*, 19 May 2022, https://www.business-standard.com/article/markets/stocks-to-watch-itc-lupin-ruchi-soya-manappuram-finance-jsw-biocon-122051900162_1.html

14 https://www.lupin.com/lupin-q1-fy2023-results/

Chapter 9: DHFL

1 2001 Annual report, https://www.bseindia.com/
   bseplus/AnnualReport/511072/5110720311.pdf; 2018
   annual report, https://www.bseindia.com/bseplus/
   AnnualReport/511072/5110720318.pdf
2 DHFL 29th annual report 2012–2013, https://
   www.dhfl.com/docs/default-source/investors/
   annual-reports/2012-2013/dhfl-ar-2012-13.pdf?
   sfvrsn=bde58962_0
3 M.G. Arjun, 'DHFL Scam | Wadhawan Brothers in
   Fraud', India Today, 11 July 2022, https://www.indiatoday.
   in/magazine/special-report/story/20220711-dhfl-scam-
   wadhawan-brothers-in-fraud-1968835-2022-07-01)
4 'DHFL Scam: The Family Accused of the Biggest Banking
   Fraud Knows How to Stay out of Jail,' The Economic
   Times, 27 June 2022, https://economictimes.indiatimes.
   com/industry/banking/finance/banking/dhfl-scam-
   the-family-accused-of-the-biggest-banking-fraud-
   knows-how-to-stay-out-of-jail/articleshow/92467586.
   cms?utm_source=contentofinterest&utm_medium=
   text&utm_campaign=cppst
5 https://www.bseindia.com/bseplus/AnnualReport/
   511072/5110720319.pdf
6 Aniruddha Bahal, 'Dewan Housing Finance Corporation
   Limited—The Anatomy of India's Biggest Financial
   Scam', 29 January 2019, https://cobrapost.com/blog/
   biggest-financial-scam/1373
7 'DHFL Scam: The Family Accused of the Biggest
   Banking Fraud Knows How to Stay out of Jail', The
   Economic Times, 27 June 2022, https://economictimes.

indiatimes.com/industry/banking/finance/banking/dhfl-scam-the-family-accused-of-the-biggest-banking-fraud-knows-how-to-stay-out-of-jail/articleshow/92467586.cms?utm_source=contentofinterest&utm_medium=text&utm_campaign=cppst

8 Business Desk, 'DHFL's Rs 34,615-Crore Fraud: A Look at India's Biggest Bank Fraud Case,' News 18, 23 June 2022, https://www.news18.com/news/business/dhfls-rs-34615-crore-fraud-a-look-at-indias-biggest-bank-fraud-case-5428069.html

9 Arjun, 'Rakesh Jhunjhunwala's Fav Mid-Cap HFC Stock Is A Strong Buy Now: Experts', rakesh-jhunjhunwala.in, 15 April 2016, https://rakesh-jhunjhunwala.in/rakesh-jhunjhunwalas-fav-mid-cap-hfc-stock-is-a-strong-buy-now-experts/

10 Ravi Dharamshi, 'Rakesh Jhunjhunwala Interview with ValueQuest – After Rupee Crisis and before 2014 Elections.' *YouTube* video, 1:01:15. 19 August 2022. https://www.youtube.com/watch?v=QaWanFCu76M

11 Interim ex parte order in the matter of Dewan Housing Finance Corporation Limited, 22 September 2020, https://www.casemine.com/judgement/in/5f86c04c342cca192e7068d2

12 ZeeBiz Web Team, 'Dewan Housing Goes Tumbling Down, Again! Guess What! Like Rakesh Jhunjhunwala, Did You Invest? See How Rich This Stock Will Make Him', Zee Biz online, 28 November 2018, https://www.zeebiz.com/india/news-rakesh-jhunjhunwala-dewan-housing-share-price-dhfl-edelweiss-phillip-capital-did-you-invest-big-bull-stocks-73401

13 ZeeBiz Web Team, 'Surprise Gift from Dewan Housing to Rakesh Jhunjhunwala, Other Investors! Shares Rocket Nearly 8 per Cent on These Reports', Zee Biz online, 19 December 2018, https://www.zeebiz.com/india/news-dewan-housing-rakesh-jhunjhunwala-stake-dhfl-share-price-8-gain-surprise-gift-for-investors-mutual-funds-business-stake-sale-76570

14 Anirudh Laskar, 'Investors to Move SC Against Plan to Delist DHFL Shares,' Livemint, 18 June 2021, https://www.livemint.com/news/india/investors-to-move-sc-against-plan-to-delist-dhfl-shares/amp-11623955779992.html

Chapter 10: A2Z Infra

1 IPO details available at https://www.chittorgarh.com/ipo/a2z_maintenance_ipo/287/
Financial details available at https://www.sebi.gov.in/sebi_data/attachdocs/1287824053650.pdf

2 'A2Z IPO: Listing Gains or Long Term Value?', Seasonal Magazine, 9 December 2010, https://www.seasonalmagazine.com/2010/12/a2z-ipo-listing-gains-or-long-term.html

3 Ministry of Power, Government of India, https://powermin.gov.in/

4 FY15 annual report of A2Z Infra, https://www.bseindia.com/bseplus/AnnualReport/533292/5332920315.pdf

5 Utpal Sheth's presentation, 'Dimensions of Mistakes in Investing' given to CFA India Society, 3 September 2022.

Chapter 11: Mandhana Retail Ventures

1 'Mandhana Industries Surges after Bombay High Court Approves Scheme of Demerger,' *Business Standard*, 1 April 2016, https://www.business-standard. com/article/markets/mandhana-industries-surges-after-bombay-high-court-approves-scheme-of-demerger-116040100267_1.html

2 2016 annual report of Mandhana Industries, financials taken from annual reports of 2006, 2016, 2007, 2008.

3 The numbers taken from annual reports but summed up by the authors (financials taken from annual reports of 2006, 2016, 2007, 2008), https://gbglobal.in/annual-reports.php

4 Harveen Ahluwalia, 'Celebrity Backed Fashion Labels Strike a Big Chord with Glamour Struck Consumers', Livemint, 1 March 2017, https://www.livemint.com/ Consumer/uhBCZvMWKcE4vjs6c8ztHL/Celebrities-association-with-fashion-labels-see-a-surge-in-I.html

5 Ibid.

6 CNBC-TV18, 'Sale Of Shares To Jhunjhunwala Will Lead To Release Of Pledged Shares: Mandhana Retail', *YouTube* video, 15 December 2016, https://www. youtube.com/watch?v=3NI2iNeSWX0

7 2018 Annual report—https://www.bseindia.com/ bseplus/annualreport/540210/5402100318.pdf; 2017 Annual report—https://www.bseindia.com/bseplus/ AnnualReport/540210/5402100317.pdf; 'How Mandhana Retail Ventures Is Making the Most of Being Human?', https://brandlicense.indianretailer.

com/archives/article/how-mandhana-retail-ventures-ismaking-the-most-of-being-human; 'Mandhana Retail Increases Sales Royalty to Salman Khan's Being Human from 3% To 5%', https://www.financialexpress.com/market/mandhana-retail-increases-sales-royalty-to-salman-khans-being-human-from-3-to-5/474882/

8 2019 Annual Report link—https://www.bseindia.com/bseplus/AnnualReport/540210/5402100319.pdf; 2020 Annual Report link—https://www.bseindia.com/bseplus/AnnualReport/540210/67473540210.pdf

9 https://www.bseindia.com/bseplus/AnnualReport/540210/67473540210.pdf

10 FY22 annual report—https://www.bseindia.com/bseplus/AnnualReport/540210/74463540210.pdf; FY21 annual report—https://www.bseindia.com/bseplus/AnnualReport/540210/71942540210.pdf

Chapter 13: Patience and a Long-Term Outlook

1 Debashis Basu, 'At 62% CAGR Over 37 Years, Rakesh Jhunjhunwala Is One of the Most Successful Investors in the World Ever', *Moneylife*, 9 September 2022, https://www.moneylife.in/article/at-62-percentage-cagr-over-37-years-rakesh-jhunjhunwala-is-one-of-the-most-successful-investors-in-the-world-ever/68304.html

2 'What Rakesh Jhunjhunwala Said on Investing through Mutual Funds,' Livemint, 19 August 2022, https://www.livemint.com/news/india/what-rakesh-jhunjhunwala-said-on-investing-through-mutual-funds-11660866522152.html